Family Adventures in Style

Falconry in Dubai.

Luxury camping, courtesy of Feather Down Farm Days.

Family Adventures in Style

Dr. Jill Nash and Carlo Nash

Inside the pod, courtesy of Whitepod, Switzerland.

Introduction

When we found out we were expecting our daughter, one of our first thoughts drifted towards travel. Naturally we thought she would just 'fit in' with our intrepid travel plans. We quickly discovered that travelling with children was a totally different ball game. Our entire travel experience had changed, packing, arriving, eating out and finding places to stay had become much more challenging. Not because our daughter was difficult – but because it is just not easy to travel with children, whatever their age. Would we change it? Not a chance.

Our travel experiences have added something special to our daughter's life, she has built up incredible social skills from constantly meeting new faces, her confidence has grown and her level of vocabulary is astonishing. Above all, we feel travelling together has brought us closer as a family and built a special bond which we wouldn't have experienced had we not had this precious time together.

The challenges we faced as travelling parents were vast and varied. From where to find a clean place to change a nappy, to entertaining in queues at the airport, and where to eat at unusual times of the day! We also quickly learnt that we had to make some important compromises; we couldn't just head off to an island we just discovered or stay out all night at a local bar. Everything had to be more planned and considered.

This is our 4th book, and in true 'luxury backpacking' style we promise to provide you with independent reviews on where to go and what to do with different ages of children. Finally, we have also included some 'close to home' options as well as some further afield destinations. However long you have together, whether it is a weekend camping in Ireland, or a year travelling South America make sure you enjoy every moment with your children and make those memories count.

Jill, Carlo & Gaia

0-3 BABY + TODDLER

3-6 PRE-SCHOOLER

7-11 JUNIOR

12-16 TEEN

What kind of family adventure would you like?

○ Action + Adventure

○ Nature + Wildlife

● Food + Discovery

● Reflect + Re-new

● Education + Hands on

● History + Culture

Preface

Young children are natural adventurers. From a child's perspective, even a simple walk down the street can be filled with exciting things to explore – perhaps a slug or a drain, puddles to jump in, walls to clamber on… Imagine throwing an exciting new location into the equation, then adding a gorgeous hotel with luxury trappings, and you have the perfect ingredients for a very memorable holiday indeed.

Travelling with children is always an adventure, in every sense of the word. Seeing the world through the wonder of your child's eyes also adds a new dimension to your own experience – it's also the ultimate family bonding opportunity. It might be a far cry from the stuff-a-few-essentials-in-the-suitcase-and-let's-wing-the-rest mentality that you enjoyed pre-children, but, with the right planning, you can still satiate your grown-up appetite for adventure whilst ensuring your child's comfort and safety. It also gives you the perfect excuse to enjoy lively activities by day, rounded off with home comforts, like delicious cuisine, relaxing deep baths to soothe body and soul, and sumptuous beds for sweet night-time slumbers at the end of the day.

And, despite what Walt Disney would have you believe, there's a great big wide world out there just waiting to be discovered. My two children Joe, six, and Grace, 15, are already veteran globetrotters. They've sat atop elephants riding through the rainforest of Elephant Hills in Phuket, spotted a Bengal tiger in Ranthambhore National Park in India, camel-trekked round the pyramids at Giza and danced with dolphins in Dubai. They've tried 4x4 scrambling in mini Land Rovers across Scottish highland estates, stroked a great tawny owl, tried their hand at falconry and watched tiny crabs scuttling across sandy beaches in the Maldives. They've stayed in stately country piles, idyllic island villas, palatial hotels and, for ultimate glamping, a giant luxury tent with golden glittering stars and tigers embroidered on the ceiling. And what do these adventures have in common? Each one has been carefully tailored to suit the needs and tastes of young children – and keep their parents pretty happy too!

The good news for intrepid families is that there are so many hotels, resorts and destinations extending their welcome to families. Make the most of the child-friendly facilities at your hotel or resort: the availability of cots, highchairs, bottle warmers and sterilizers means less packing for you. Children's clubs and baby-sitting facilities also means some dedicated grown-up time, should you wish to treat yourself to a pampering spa treatment or a romantic dinner a deux, safe in the knowledge that your children are having fun, too. After all, a happy holiday means taking into account everyone's pleasure and leisure requirements. Here's to happy, and stylish, family adventures!

Catherine O'Dolan
Editor-in-Chief
Junior Magazine

www.juniormagazine.co.uk

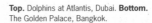
Top. Dolphins at Atlantis, Dubai. **Bottom.** The Golden Palace, Bangkok.

🛏 Top 3 Travel Tips for Families

1. Make life as comfortable and easy as possible by choosing a climate that will suit your family – mild and dry is best (for both sunny and ski destinations) so avoid sweltering or f-f-f-freezing temperatures, and rainy monsoon seasons, where possible. Unless, of course, you're venturing into a rainforest, in which case, dramatic downpours are all part of the adventure! Jet lag is another consideration, especially if your child is a haphazard sleeper at the best of times.

2. Take your child on a virtual learning adventure of your destination before you set off on your travels, checking out what sights you might see and what foods you might eat. Learn a little of the local lingo, too, so you can greet the locals with a few words – they will always appreciate it, especially if it is delivered by a cute toddler!

3. Encourage your child's wanderlust by giving her a camera and a travel journal so she can keep a diary of her travels. Collect postcards, sweet wrappers and any interesting memorabilia – it will make a wonderful keepsake, and these souvenirs can be turned into an impressive 'Show-and-Tell' back in the classroom.

For more tips on family travel, visit
www.juniormagazine.co.uk

Petting cows, courtesy of Feather Down Farm Days.

IRELAND + NORTHERN IRELAND

Co Dublin | Co Mayo | Co Cork | Northern Ireland

🏆 Why is this place so special?

Ireland is an ideal country for families with children of all ages; with its vast open countryside, camping farms, and medieval castles - it is simply a fairy-tale playground for kids. If that's not enough then Celtic mysticism, leprechauns and shamrocks, will soon engage a young enquiring mind.

Ireland has a varied landscape, and within a few miles; you can travel from rugged coastline to pastureland and historical sites. You can spend the night anywhere from an ancient castle to a luxury campsite; dine on fine Irish cuisine or snack on fish and chips. The sheer number of sights, villages, charming pubs, and adorable restaurants can seem often overwhelming. It is practical, easy to get around, friendly and if you happen to be travelling from the UK – it is very accessible by plane or ferry.

Visiting Ireland's cosmopolitan cities such as Dublin is a real treat for children. Offering everything from open-top bus tours of the city, to Irish dancing and not forgetting the 'Dublinia' - an exhibition on medieval life, where young ones can loose themselves in the viking and medieval world.

County Mayo is the place for the family outdoors; learn to surf, sail, and climb or take a picnic in the woods. A visit to Westport House (with an adjoining water park) hosts many festivals and events throughout the year and equally has a number of blue flag beaches which are perfect for the summer.

One of the best parts of the country for those travelling with kids is arguably Cork where everything seems to be set up for families. Kiss the bluestone at Blarney Castle (said to give you the gift of eloquence) and experience a wooden cable car to Dursey Island or treat your kids to a 'children's afternoon tea' at Hayfield Manor.

Finally, last but certainly not least is stunning Northern Ireland. Although it shares a border with Ireland is actually one of the four countries which make up the UK. With its improved international reputation it is fast becoming a tourist hotspot. Children will simply love uncovering the amazing story of 'Titanic' at the Ulster folk museum or discovering the geological phenomenon, 'Giants Causeway' on the North Antrim coast. Families who love nature and wildlife can experience staying on a real working farm (in a luxury tent of course) where young ones can 'hire' rabbits, lambs and feed chickens for a week.

Family life is very important in Irish culture and so taking the kids with you to most restaurants, sights, and even pubs (during the day) is never a problem. Whether you are planning on a long weekend, a week or two, then Ireland definitely has enough to keep the whole family entertained without necessarily breaking the bank.

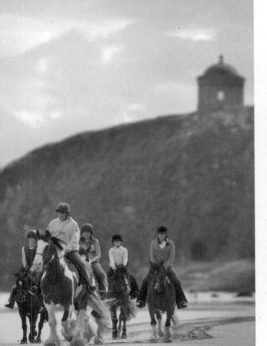

📖 Fun Facts

Capitals: Dublin is the capital of Ireland, while Belfast is the capital of Northern Ireland.

Population: 4,062,235 (Ireland) 1,799,000 (Northern Ireland)

Currency: The Euro is the currency of Ireland, while the Pound Sterling is used in Northern Ireland.

Languages: Irish Gaelic, English.

Trivia: Did you know... there are no wild snakes in Ireland? The sea has stopped many animals common on mainland Europe from reaching the island.

Getting there and exploring around

Low cost airlines have made it fairly cheap and easy to fly to Ireland from the UK and continent. Ferries are a valid (and fun) alternative for families travelling from England, Scotland and France. A variety of ferry services including Brittany Ferries, Isle of Man Steam Packet, Stena Line, Irish Ferries, P&O Irish Sea and Swansea - Cork Ferries operate regular sailings to Ireland.

Ireland has several ports with ferry connections to the Isle of Man, Wales and France. The shortest crossings from the UK are from Holyhead, in Northern Wales, to either Dublin or Dun Laoghaire (just south of Dublin). Ferries also run from Liverpool to Dublin. From southern England, you may prefer a new ferry route that's opened from Swansea to Cork - a great jumping off point for Ireland's famed southwest coast. Other UK crossings are from Fishguard, Wales to Rosslare, in the southeast corner of Ireland, and to Belfast from either the Isle of Man or Liverpool. The French ports of Cherbourg and Roscoff also offer connections to Rosslare and Cork.

The best way to travel Ireland is hire a car as it offers the greatest independence, and if booked in advance can offer child rear and facing seats. The Republic of Ireland has an extensive bus network making bus travel a good budget option. Travel by train is pleasurable but the limited rail system only connects the main cities. The Luas, (a light rail tram system), makes getting round Dublin quick and easy. Taxis are readily available in the principal cities, but may not offer car seats for small children.

Best time of year to visit

Would you rather gaze at the rainbows that show up during the spring in Ireland, or enjoy the solitude of the countryside during the winter? Do your kids want to learn to surf on a beach? Should you base yourself in one place and take day trips, or go the nomadic route? It is almost impossible to suggest a 'best time' to visit Ireland, because it is really a 'year round' destination offering something for everyone at different times of the year. Obviously it goes without saying that the summer (May-August) is arguably the best time because temperatures are warm and towns are brimming with life and attractions are open for longer, making outdoor adventures possible for families. Spring can also be beautiful, flowers are in blossom and it's the time of year when the Irish celebrate 'Saint Patrick's' day. Needles to say, that if you are travelling from the UK then Ireland can be visited throughout the year. I.e. you don't necessarily have to wait until the 'school holidays' as it is popular and accessible for weekend trips.

FUN FAMILY FACT:

An odd Irish birthday tradition is to lift the birthday child upside down and give his head a few gentle bumps on the floor for good luck. The number of bumps should allegedly correspond to the child's age plus one.

? Must know before you go

Let's have a 'craic'. Craic is the Gaelic term for 'fun', or to generally mean having a good time. You'll hear it everywhere, so if a local asks you if you're having a 'craic', don't be offended or confuse it with the illegal narcotic substance.

Gaeltacht towns. If you're hiring a car then most road signs in Ireland are in Irish and English. In a few Irish-speaking (Gaeltacht) areas, they're in Irish only. As Ireland is currently migrating to the metric system, you'll see new green and white signs in kilometres, along with older black and white signs calibrated in miles.

Weather for all seasons. Pack for all seasons in summer. Pack rain gear and plan to dress in layers whether travelling in June or January. It is also a good idea to pack a lightweight stroller if you have toddlers whose legs might get tired while sightseeing. If you are planning more intrepid walks then a solid ATP (all-terrain pushchair) or a framed child carrier are invaluable.

 Highlights

Dublinia Heritage Centre. Situated in the heart of Dublin this exciting heritage centre has 3 exhibitions which will guarantee to entertain and educate the whole family.

Surfing & Sailing. Hire a boat in Clew Bay (County Mayo) and follow the footsteps of great pirates, or learn to surf at sandy Enniscrone beach (County Sligo) just outside County Mayo.

Picnic Time. Pack a picnic lunch and head to Blarney Castle (County Cork), a 600-year old castle with beautiful gardens and lots of walks.

The Great Outdoors. Camping at Feather Down Farm days and exploring Ireland's world heritage site the mesmerizing 'Giants Causeway.'

👍 Tip for the Trip

"Getting your children started on a few holiday-related projects before you leave is a great way to prepare them for what's in store. You could explore maps, music, history, geography and wildlife of your destination, or read books or watch a film that is set there. If the food is likely to be radically different, research dishes that they might enjoy, and try preparing something similar before you go."

Adventure: History + Culture
Destination: County Dublin

✈ Regional Information

Dublin ranks among the top tourist destinations in Europe and in the last decade there
has been an economic boom, which has seen areas of Dublin change dramatically.
Many historical areas have been restored; new shopping centres have arrived along
with restaurants and small hotels making this a very exciting place to visit. For families
there are plenty of attractions and monuments to keep little ones amused, especially
between the ages of 3-11.

Some of the best known monuments and landmarks include the Dublin National
Museum, Castletown House, the National Gallery, St. Patrick's Cathedral, Custom
House and Christ Church Cathedral – depending on the age of your children – are
centrally located and are well worth a visit.

Dublinia is a heritage centre located in the heart of the medieval city of Dublin.
There are three exciting exhibitions to see. Viking Dublin takes you back to life in the
city in Viking times; the Medieval Dublin exhibition includes a busy medieval market,
a rich merchant's house, and a noisy medieval street; and History Hunters brings the
exhibitions full circle. This interactive centre is a perfect option for rainy days.

Another rainy day option is Imaginosity, the Dublin Children's Museum - a unique
child-orientated creative space for children up to 9 years of age, and their families.
Imaginosity's 2.5 floors of exhibits are educationally designed to inspire life-long
learning through play, celebrating children's imaginations on the journey from curiosity
to discovery. Become a mechanic in The Garage, examine an x-ray in Dr. Apple-a-Day's
Surgery, choose the evening meal in the Village Market and cook it up at the Dublin Diner.
Sing, dance and dress-up in costumes in The Theatre or present the News at the TV
Station or become an engineer in the construction zone. The opportunities are endless.

Adventure: History + Culture
Destination: County Dublin

For sunny days head to Dublin's Phoenix Park. It is vast and twice the size of New York's Central Park and almost five times as large as London's Hyde Park. It is home to many attractions, including the Irish White House - official residence of the Irish president, the incredibly tall Wellington Monument, and large areas of open parkland, with ideal spots for relaxing picnics, a stroll or for burning off energy. Getting around the city is easy, and like most cities in the world there is a 'Sightseeing hop on/off' open top bus which is a fun way to see the city. The tour stops in over 27 places around the city and children go free – which is an added bonus in an expensive city.

Dublin was originally called 'Dubh Linn,' which means 'Black Pool' in Irish. The name refers to an ancient treacle lake in the city, which is now part of a penguin enclosure at the Dublin city zoo. No trip to Dublin would be complete without a visit to Ireland's No.1 visitor attraction. As one of the world's oldest and most popular zoos, the 70-acre park in the heart of Dublin is home to some 600 animals in an environment where education and conservation combine for an exciting and unforgettable experience. See many rare and exotic animals living and roaming a wide variety of natural habitats. Wander through the African Savanna and gaze at the giraffes, zebras, scimitar oryx and ostrich, then head to the Kaziranga Forest to see the magnificent herd of Asian elephants that call this beautiful place home. Experience the heat of the South American House before heading to Family Farm and don't forget to visit the soon to be opened Gorilla Rainforest.

For evening entertainment then look no further than the 'Irish House Party'. It is the only venue in Dublin that allows children with their parents to experience traditional Irish music and dancing. The dinner seating is at 7pm and the show finishes at 10pm (so bear this in mind with young ones who need their sleep). Set in a magnificent 18th townhouse, The Irish House Party is dinner and traditional Irish entertainment with a twist. It is both a musical and dance celebration where parents can also join in to dance or just sit back.

In a recent survey, Dublin appeared in the top ten of the world's most liveable cities. The friendly, hospitable nature of the people that live here, together with the beautiful setting and easy accessibly, all contribute to this being a great family destination, whether you have a couple of days or longer.

Places to Stay

Brooks Hotel

Brooks is located on Drury Street, within a few minutes from Dublin's famed Grafton Street. The hotel has a succinct air of sophistication with tastefully furnished rooms and modern works of art. It has a gorgeous panelled resident's lounge complete with an impressive library, free Wifi, and fresh organic produce is used in their restaurant.

Guide Price: From £100 prpn
Best Room: One bedroom suite with separate lounge area for the kids

Dylan Hotel

Located in a non-touristy Dublin neighbourhood yet only a 15 minute walk to the centre of town. Packed with all modern amenities from IPOD stereo system, B&O cordless phones to free Wifi. The very helpful and knowledgeable concierge also provides maps and recommend places to eat and explore in the city. The hotel features huge family rooms with fabulous decor and rollaway cots for little ones. Brownies and bedtime snacks at turndown service.

Guide Price: From £150 prpn
Best Room: Dylan Experience

The K Club

Staying on the luxurious, grand estate encompasses everything that is Ireland. Located in Kildare near Dublin City, the atmosphere is opulent yet relaxed, with reminders of Yeats and Irish history decorating every room. It has fabulous spacious grounds with a variety of walks and gardens for picnics. Children are well catered for with lots of exciting outdoor activities such as free bicycles, swimming lessons, archery and fly fishing.

Guide Price: From £200 prpn
Best Room: Book one of the refurbished deluxe rooms, for more space and modern amenities

Places to Eat

Gallagher's Boxty House, Dublin City

A traditional Irish pub, right in the centre of 'Temple bar'. They are known for their inventive pancakes, friendly Irish hospitality and a good variety of children's dishes. As well as Boxty pancakes Gallagher's Boxty House also serves stews, steaks, seafood and vegetarian dishes. Great for lunch or an evening meal.

The Ceder Tree, Dublin City

A bustling middle-eastern restaurant, serving Lebanese food. They have an excellent variety of traditional 'mezes' (great for a family sharing) and side dishes such as lentil soups, grilled halloumi, and hummous. The shishtaouk (marinated chicken) kebabs are delicious, as are the kafta halabieh (chargrilled meatballs of minced lamb, parsley, pine nuts and onion). Byblos 'house of mezze' next door is under the same ownership and serves lighter meals throughout the day. Good value for money luncheon spot.

Cruzzo, Malahide

Great fish restaurant located in the heart of the Malahide Marina amid the moored majestic white yachts. A fabulous spot for children who love boats, and they can burn off some energy walking around the marina. From the grill there is a selection of steaks, a surf and turf option and the fab sounding grilled skewer of tiger prawns with spiced aubergine, mint and honey yoghurt. They have early bird menus and serve excellent fishcakes for children.

Adventure:
Action + Adventure
Destination: County Mayo

IDEAL FOR
ALL
AGES

✦ Regional Information

Mayo is Ireland's third largest county, boasting a beautiful coastline and picturesque villages of Ballina, Castlebar and Westport. The River Moy, renowned for its famous salmon fishing sweeps the north-east corner while Clew Bay (a natural ocean) defines the south-west.

Families who love action and adventure won't be short of things to do in this county. Starting with the north-east corner, Ballina is a great base to stay to enjoy the beautiful surroundings of the coastline. Nearby beautiful beaches Enniscrone, Ross & Killala offer an abundance of activities from learning to surf to horse riding.

Enniscrone Beach is an idyllic location which has over two miles of excellent surfing conditions suitable for the novice and intermediate surfer. Two surf schools offer a safe and enjoyable environment with surfboards and wet suits provided. During the summer months there are 'surf' camps for children and their parents. 'Iceford Stables', situated 3.5 kilometres from Enniscrone offer pony camps, beach rides for both groups and private lessons – a great experience for juniors and teenagers.

For smaller children 'Belleek Woods' is a lovely woodland walking area, situated along the banks of the River Moy. It is an ideal place to explore the woodlands, bogs, wildlife – and a popular duck pond. There are also plenty of picnic areas to feed tired and hungry children. For rainy days an interesting place to visit is the 'Foxford Woollen Mill' which has a good interactive visitor's experience, explaining the story of local nuns who established the mill during hardened times. The mill also has a lovely shop, selling home interiors and children's products, and a café, selling local homemade food.

Adventure: Action + Adventure
Destination: County Mayo

Further afield, lays the pretty town of Westport. A quaint town renowned for Westport House - Ireland's most significant historical home and premier visitor experience. Built in 1730 on the ruins of a previous castle of legendary Pirate Queen Grace O'Malley – and complete with original architecture, antiques, and dungeons, wax work displays and exhibitions – it is home to her direct descendants. Stunning scenery, architectural magnificence, beautifully manicured gardens and a Pirate Adventure Park combine with a remarkable history is a memorable, awe-inspiring and fun experience for all age groups.

Clew Bay itself is home to many outdoor activities from bike riding, to wind surfing and sea kayaking. There are plenty of designated bicycle trails for different levels in Westport, Clare Island and Achill Island. Clew Bay outdoors centre can supply all the equipment you may need including helpful maps of the area.

The village of Cong, which lies further south, is home to 12th century Cong Abbey, Ashford Castle, Cong Wood - and is also known as the filming location of the 'Quiet Man' starring John Wayne. The villagers remember the making of the film as a momentous event which brought world-wide attention to their walled fields and old-fashioned pubs. Although you can retrace the steps of the actors throughout the town, there is much more to Cong than just a movie set. The village is small and intimate with excellent pubs and not withstanding lovely walks around the Abbey, Ashford castle (half an hour from medieval city of Galway) offers exciting family activities from horse-riding, falconry to clay pigeon shooting. One of the highlights of staying here is experiencing the 'lake cruise', its excellent value for money as it is led by a local historian and the cruise takes you on a voyage of discovery to the island of St. Patrick, and the monastic site on Inchagoill Island.

Families have such a choice of wonderful places to stay in County Mayo, from picturesque castles to refurbished riverside ice houses, children (or their parents) won't be disappointed.

 Places to Stay

Clew Bay Hotel

A family-owned 3 star hotel situated in the centre of Westport. It is a good choice for families as it is located near to Westport House & the Adventure Park and also conveniently located within walking distance from many restaurants and shops.

Guide Price: From £100 prpn
Best Room: A family room with a double bed and two singles

Ice House

A stunning boutique hotel situated on the banks of the River Moy in Ballina. This hotel used to be an 'ice store' for local fisherman and has kept its unique character but been modernised to the highest standards. There is also a small children play room with a Wii, a stunning spa (with outdoor hot tubs) for parents to chill.

Guide price: From £120 prpn
Best Room: Book the spacious 'spa suite' with separate living area

Ashford Castle

For over 700 years, Ashford Castle and its 350 acre private estate have offered a real Irish experience. The hotel offers 'hawk walks' as well as many other activities to keep families entertained. Children under 2 receive a teddy, baby pack and ducks for the bath, and for over 2's a bathrobe, slippers, and chocolates.

Guide Price: From £300 prpn
Best Room: Book the 'stateroom' for space and an authentic experience

Places to Eat

Foxford Mill Café, Nr Ballina

A great spot for lunch, serving organic fresh produce, cakes, smoothies and fresh pastries. Even better if you are just driving through and can buy a picnic or take-away.

Enoteca, Westport

Robert and Andrea are charming hosts, serving great, hearty Italian and seafood cuisine. Scallops on butternut squash and rosemary puree, and carpaccio of beef are clear favourites for the entrée and lobster risotto and parcel of sea bass for main course. Highly recommend.

Cullens at the Cottage, Ashford Castle

A thatched cottage within sight of the castle, Cullen's at The Cottage is named after the late Peter Cullen, a much-loved former Maitre D', and offers a completely different experience: mid-priced dining, open to the public, with none of the pomp and ceremony associated with the grandeur of meals served in the castle itself. Dining can be 'al fresco' in the summer months.

Adventure:
Food + Discovery
Destination: County Cork

✈ Regional Information

County Cork is situated in the South West of Ireland, it is the largest of all the Irish counties and in many ways the most varied. Rich farmlands and river valleys contrast with the wild sandstone hills of the west, and above all there is the magnificent coastline scooped and fretted by the Atlantic into great bays and secret coves, strewn with rocky headlands and long soft golden sands. Cork has been named as one of the world top 10 cities to visit by many, and it is not hard to see why.

Cork is a very cool and laid back city, from play zones to prisons, it offers a variety of experiences to keep little ones happy. A stroll through the pretty city to visit Shandon Church which stands tall and proud over the city is a must. You can even climb the 120ft steeple to ring the bells of Shandon and gaze at the panoramic views of the city.

Afterwards, you can all go shopping at the 'English market' (located on Grand parade) a municipal gourmet food market where you can pick up local produce (or even a picnic) and take a trip to Kinsdale, where there is a beautiful harbour and you can pick up a boat and see seals, herons and plenty of wildlife. Cork city also offers plenty to keep the family occupied on rainy days, with cinemas, indoor play areas and novel child friendly museums such as the pleasantly scary exhibition Cork City Gaol, which is a heritage centre and radio museum with wax figurines of prisoners. Also Lifetime Lab a modern interactive exhibition, steam plant, beautifully restored buildings, children's playground and marvellous views over the River Lee.

The Opera House and Everyman Palace Theatre run a diverse programme of music, plays, and dance throughout the year. With a number of annual Cork festivals, such as The Jazz Festival, Cork Arts Festival, and the Film Festival, it is clear to see why Cork was the European Capital of Culture in 2005. Over 150 years old, the Cork Opera House offers a world-class programme of events across all disciplines in the performing arts. It's Cork's premier venue and boasts a 1,000 seat auditorium, and has a wide variety of plays and pantomimes for families.

Adventure: Food + Discovery
Destination: County Cork

A little further from Cork city is Blarney Castle, where you can easily fill an entire afternoon kissing rocks, climbing castle walls, and exploring Badger Cave and the castle's gloomy dungeons. The sprawling grounds make a perfect place to dine alfresco. The village of Blarney is a must – see for any visitor to Cork. Stroll through the stunning gardens of the Blarney Castle, and take the opportunity to kiss the legendary Blarney Stone, which will bestow you with the gift of eloquence. For a unique shopping excursion, visit the Blarney Woollen Mills which specializes in Irish gifts and souvenirs. End the day with a taste of Irish cuisine in one of the many pubs and restaurants surrounding the village green.

For families who love their food, a trip to the 'East Cork Food Trail' is a must. The rich resources of the surrounding countryside and superb atlantic seafood, the farmer's markets, speciality food shops and a fine selection of dining facilities offer visitors a wonderful gourmet experience on this trail. You will have the opportunity to visit and experience places such as the Midleton farmers market, one of the oldest in Ireland, and the world famous Ballymaloe Cookery School & Gardens as well as some fine artisan food producers.

Located on the southwestern tip of county Cork is Dursey Island. Take the family on an unforgettable ride in a cable car out to the island, which you can easily explore on foot while taking in the sweeping views. Back on the mainland there are plenty of little colourful towns, including Ballydehob, where all the signs for local shops and pubs are done in pictures rather than words. Take them to the Drombeg Stone Circle to learn about ancient religions; its strange beauty will bewitch even younger travellers.

An hour's drive away in a western direction from Cork city is Inchydony island. For children who love to run on long white beaches and dig sandcastles, this spot is idyllic. The generous beach here has achieve a 'blug flag' status and there are an abundance of activities from kayaking to whale watching.

Places to Stay

Inchydoney Island Lodge
Situated on the idyllic island of Inchydoney, adjacent to a stunning EU Blue Flag beach, this luxurious hotel offers deluxe rooms, a fully equipped thalassotherapy (seawater) spa, award-winning restaurant and a relaxed Dunes pub & bistro. Its no surprise this place has won many travel awards.
Guide Price: From £120 prpn
Best Room: Book a deluxe ocean suite with a terrace overlooking the sea

Hayfield Manor
Rooms are fully equipped in grand style, from the opulent drapes at the windows, king sized beds and comfy armchairs, to the fluffy robes and slippers in the bathrooms, which come complete with traditional and roomy roll top baths and Elemis toiletries. There is a DVD library for the perfect movie night in, complete with popcorn! Cookies & milk at bedtime for children.
Guide Price: From £200 prpn
Best Room: Executive suite with views across the gardens

Castelmartyr Resort
A stately 17th century manor, nestled in a 220 acres of private woodland. Kids can enjoy the exciting activities in our Kids Zone, enjoy their own splash times in the indoor pool or even take Earl & Countess (the resident Irish Setters) for a walk.
Guide Price: From £200 prpn
Best Room: For a family of four, two-bed suites are the ideal family accommodation

Places to Eat

Strasbourg Goose, Cork
A cosy family owned restaurant in the heart of Cork city at the Huguenot Quarter. Offers excellent quality cuisine (all dishes are made from scratch) at reasonable prices. Book ahead as it can get busy at the weekends.

Le Voyage, Skibbereen
Serving European and traditional Irish cuisine, Le Voyage has a great local reputation. The restaurant is lovely, bright and delightful, and the staff are very welcoming. They have an excellent variety of children's dishes from melon balls to daily specials.

Market Lane, Cork
In the heart of Cork. Market Lane is an award winning restaurant and bar over two floors. Ingredients used are from the English Market and local artisan producers, to make up the menu which has a wide range of fish, salads, meat, game and sandwiches. In addition there are coeliac and vegetarian dishes and a healthy kids menu.

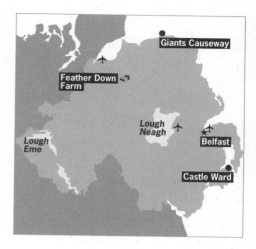

Focus On...
Northern Ireland

Following many turbulent years of civil unrest, Northern Ireland is fast becoming a European 'hotspot' for tourists. It's fabulous landscapes, countryside and history is alluring travellers globally.

Northern Ireland is probably most recognised internationally as the destination where the famous HMS Titanic was built. When Titanic sailed away on her maiden voyage on April 10th, 1912, she was hailed as 'the new wonder of the world'. A remarkable feat of engineering, she was the largest and most luxuriously appointed ship ever seen and, despite her tragic sinking five days later, she remains a source of enduring pride in the city where she was built - Belfast. Today stands a major exhibition at the 'Ulster Folk & Transport Museum' of 500 original artefacts, including Titanic objects recovered from the icy Atlantic. There is also a fun 'people story' experience which visitors can walk the historic streets and meet the people who built the ship and lived in her time. Chat to the shipyard Riveter in his house, visit Baird's Print Shop to get your own Titanic launch ticket or dress up in costume of the time for a family photo with a difference. An extra big bag of sweets will be needed from the old style Corner Shop before heading to the Picture House to enjoy Titanic related films.

One of Northern Irelands most stunning natural features is 'The Giant's Causeway', situated on the North East coast, and is an area of about 40,000 interlocking basalt columns, the result of an ancient volcanic eruption. A UNESCO world heritage site with a beautiful coastal path extending 11 miles, located in County Antrim on the northeast coast, about three miles (4.8 kilometres) northeast of the town of Bushmills.
It is an intriguing site for children (and their imaginations), as they will enjoy learning about the Irish warrior allegedly built the causeway to walk to Scotland.

Castle Ward located in County Down, is an 18th-century eccentric house with two distinctly different styles, classical and Gothic, This truly beautiful 332-hectare (820-acre) walled garden, with walking trails, exotic garden, stunning vistas and picturesque farmyard, will unlock your imagination through family history, leisure pursuits, events and industrial heritage.

For a unique family experience stay at the impressive 'Feather Down Farm', a 13th generation family run farm, located in Dungiven. This is the ultimate 'outdoor camping experience' for families who love to camp without the hassle of packing a tent and a car full of equipment. The 'tents' are bed ready, with beds, duvets, and they offer real experiences such as campfires and soup & stew over a wood burning stove.

ⓘ Stylish Essentials

General Information

Discover Ireland
General Tourist information
www.discoverireland.ie

Dublin
Official Tourist Office
www.visitdublin.com
T. +353 (0) 1605 7700

County Mayo
www.mayo.ie

County Cork
www.visitcorkcounty.com

Trains

Luas Tram
info@luas.ie
www.luas.ie

Ferry's

Brittany Ferries
www.brittanyferries.com
T. 0871 244 0744 (UK reservations)
customer.feedback@brittanyferries.com

Stena Line
www.stenaline.co.uk
T. 08447 70 70 70 (UK reservations)

Irish Ferries
www.irishferries.com
T. +353 (0) 818 300 400
(reservations)

Airlines

Aer Lingus
www.aerlingus.com
T. 0871 718 2020 (UK reservations)

Ryanair
www.ryanair.com
T. 0871 246 0000 (UK reservations)

Jet2
www.jet2.com
T. 0871 226 1737 (UK reservations)

County Dublin

Dublin Zoo
Dublin 8
www.dublinzoo.ie
T. +353 (0) 1474 8900
E. info@dublinzoo.ie

Dublinia
St. Michael's Hill,
Christchurch, Dublin 8
www.dublinia.ie
T. +353 (0) 1679 4611
E. info@dublinia.ie

The Plaza
Beacon South Quarter,
Sandyford, Dublin 18
www.imaginosity.ie
T. +353 (0) 1217 6130
E. info@imaginosity.ie

Phoenix Park
Dublin 8
www.heritageireland.ie/en/
historicsites
T. +353 (0) 1677 0095
E. phoenixparkvisitorcentre@opw.ie

The Irish House Party
Suite 401
22/23 Pembroke Street Upper
www.theirishhouseparty.com
T. +353 (0) 1661 8410

Dylan Hotel
Eastmoreland Place
Dublin 4,
www.dylan.ie
T. +353 (0) 1660 3000

Brooks Hotel
Dublin City Centre
59-63 Drury Street, Dublin
www.brookshotel.ie
T. +353 (0) 1670 4000

The K Club
Straffan,
Co. Kildare, Ireland
www.kclub.ie
T. +353 (0) 1601 7200

Boxty House
20-21 Temple Bar,
Dublin 2
www.boxtyhouse.ie
T. +353 (0) 1677 2762
Open: Mon to Thu,Sun 10.00–23.00,
Fri 10.00–23.30 & Sat 9.00–23:30

Ceder Tree
11a Saint Andrews Street,
Dublin 2
T. +353 (0) 1677 2121
Open: Mon to Sat 12.00–23.30 &
Sun 14.00–22.00

Cruzzo
Marina Village
Malahide
Co. Dublin
www.cruzzo.ie
T. +353 (0) 1845 0599
E. info@cruzzo.ie
Open: Lunch Tues to Sat
12.00–15.00, Sun 12.00–16.00.
Dinner Tues to Fri 18.00–22.00 &
Sat 18.00–22.30

County Mayo

Surf School
Atlantic Surf School
www.atlanticsurfschool.com
T. +353 (0) 87 959 55 56
E.info@nwsurfschool.com

Horse Riding
Iceford Stables
www.icefordstables.com
T. +353 (0) 96 70776

Enniscrone Beach
www.discoverenniscrone.com

Foxford Woollen Mill
Foxford,
Co. Mayo,
www.foxfordwoollenmills.com
T. +353 (0) 94 9256104

Westport House
Westport House & Pirate Adventure
Park,
Westport,
Co Mayo
www.westporthouse.ie
T. +353 (0) 98 27766

Clew Bay Bike Hire & Outdoors
Distillery Road Westport
Ireland
www.clewbayoutdoors.ie
T. +353 (0) 98 24818
E. info@clewbayoutdoors.ie

Ice House
The Quay
Ballina,
Co. Mayo
www.icehousehotel.ie
T. +353 (0) 96 23 500

Clew Bay Hotel
James St, Westport,
Co. Mayo
www.clewbayhotel.com
T. +353 (0) 98 28088

Ashford Castle
Cong,
Co Mayo, Ireland
www.ashford.ie
T. +353 (0) 94 9546003

Enoteca
Market Lane,
Westport, Ireland
T. +353 (0) 87 2793368
Open: Tues to Sat 17.30–21.30

Cullen's at The Cottage
Ashford Castle
Co Mayo
T. + 353 (0) 94 9546003
Open: 11.00–21.30 Mon to Sun

County Cork

Cork City Gaol
Convent Avenue
Cork, Co. Cork, Ireland
www.corkcitygaol.com
T. +353 (0) 21 430 5022

Lifetime Lab
Lee Road,
Cork.
www.lifetimelab.ie
T. +353 (0) 21 494 1500

Cork Opera House
1 Emmet Place
Cork, Co. Cork, Ireland
www.corkoperahouse.ie
T. +353 (0) 21 427 0022

Everyman Palace Theatre
15 MacCurtain Street, Cork
www.everymanpalace.com
T. +353 (0) 21 450 1673

Blarney Castle
www.blarneycastle.ie
T. +353 (0) 21 438 5252
E. info@blarneycastle.ie

Midleton Farmers Market
Hospital Road
This Farmers Market is held the on
Saturdays, from 10.00–14.00

**Ballymaloe Cookery School
& Gardens**
Ballymaloe Cookery School
Shanagarry
Co. Cork
T. + 353 (0) 21 4646785

Hayfield Manor
Hayfield Manor Hotel, Perrott Avenue,
College Road
Cork City
www.hayfieldmanor.ie
T. + 353 (0) 21 484 5900
E. enquiries@hayfieldmanor.ie

Castlemartyr Resort
www.castlemartyrresort.ie
T. +353 (0) 214219000

Inchydoney Island Lodge
Inchydoney Island Lodge & Spa
Clonakilty,
West Cork
www.inchydoneyisland.com
T. +353 (0) 23 8833143

Strasbourg Goose
17/18 French Church Street
Cork
www.strasbourggoosecork.com
T. +353 (0) 21 427 9534
Open: Tue to Fri 17.30 – late, Sat &
Sun 12.00 – late

Le Voyage
73 Bridge Street,
Skibbereen,
Co. Cork
www.levoyage.ie
T. +353 (0) 28 23112
E. info@levoyage.ie

Market Lane
5/6 Oliver Plunkett St
Cork City
www.marketlane.ie
T. +353 (0) 21 4274710

Northern Ireland

Feather Down Farm Days
Ash Park Farm,
Dungiven
County Derry
www.featherdown.co.uk
T. +44 (0) 1420 80804
(UK reservations)

Titanica The Exhibition
Ulster Folk & Transport Museum,
Holywood, Co Down
BT18 0EU
www.nmni.com

Castle Ward
Strangford, Downpatrick,
County Down
BT30 7LS
www.nationaltrust.org.uk/castleward

Giants Causeway
44a Causeway Road, Bushmills,
County Antrim BT57 8SU
www.nationaltrust.org.uk/
main/w-giantscauseway
T. +353 (0) 28 2073 1582

White Turf, St Moritz.

SWITZERLAND

Valais | St. Moritz |
Jungfrau & Interlaken | Zürich

🏆 Why is this place so special?

Switzerland is celebrated for its high quality of life, sophisticated ski resorts, luxurious watches, and not forgetting its delicious chocolate and cheese. Nestled at the centre of Europe and featuring the highest peaks of the Alps, Switzerland is a country of striking nature. As a relatively small country it is a great destination for a family trip, and children will be spoilt for choice for things to do.

Mountains occupy at least 60% of Swiss land, so there are a multitude of sports for both winter and summer, like climbing, ice climbing, glacier walking, snow boarding, snow golf, dog-sledding, and heli-skiing. Switzerland has some of the best skiing in Europe and the world class regions Berner Oberland, Graubunden and Valais offer skiing at different levels. If all that proves too much with little ones, then you can head to one of the stunning cities, such as Interlaken or Zürich, explore the history, take a boat ride on a lake and just marvel at the snow-capped mountain ranges from a distance. If you are heading for summer sunshine, then the classy town of St. Moritz which enjoys 322 days of sun per year, offering beautiful walks, horse-back riding and not forgetting the famous 'Heidi Museum' - it is a superb choice for a family summer holiday.

Interestingly Switzerland also showcases three of Europe's most distinctive cultures, which gives the country lots of intrigue. To the northeast is Swiss-German-speaking Switzerland; to the southwest you find wine drinking French style; in the southéast, south of the Alps, the sun warms Italian-style piazzas; and in the centre lies classic Swiss flugelhorns and mountain landscapes. So every region offers completely different experiences, yet it always feels unified with a unique sense of 'Swissness.'

Switzerland is naturally famous for its mouth-watering variety of chocolates and cheeses. A specialty is fondue, a delicious hot concoction of Gruyère and Vacherin cheese, melted and mixed with white wine, flour, Kirsch and a little garlic. Once a

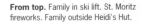

peasants dish, (they used to dip in stale bread) it is renowned across all of Switzerland (especially in the ski resorts) and is a popular eating experience for children who like to 'dip their food'. Chocolate, the nation's favourite sweet treat, is synonymous with Switzerland. Swiss chocolate is particularly famous for its smooth texture and refined taste. Milk chocolate, a Swiss invention, is famous because of the cream and milk derived from Swiss cows. Chocolate tourism is massive in Switzerland and there are plenty of experiences and activities for children such as the 'chocolate train' and visiting the famous 'Lindt chocolate shop'.

In terms of accommodation there are plenty of choices, from charming small hotels to grand castles, cosy ski lodges or eco-chic hillside tents. There is something for every taste and budget.

If you are flying from Europe, Switzerland can be a glorious trip for a family weekend, or longer if you have packed your hiking boots or ski's, or you can incorporate it with a European adventure and tie-in France and Germany too.

🗎 Fun Facts

Capital: Bern.

Population: 7,785,800.

Currency: Swiss Franc.

Languages: German, French, Italian, Rumantsch.

Trivia: There is no Swiss language. Depending on where you are in the country the locals might speak Swiss-German (Schwyzerdütsch), French, Italian, or, in the hidden valleys of Graubünden, Romansch, an ancient language related to Latin.

Getting there and exploring around

Depending on where you are travelling from, flying is probably the most favoured method. With the emergence of 'low cost' budget airlines in Europe (for example, BMI, Easyjet), Switzerland has never been easier to get to.

The major international airports are in Zürich, Geneva and Basel, with smaller airports in Lugano and Berne. The flag carrier of Switzerland is SWISS which is a member of Star Alliance and successor of the famous Swissair.

Trains arriving from all parts of Europe connect to Switzerland, and is together with Germany one of the most central-lying countries in Europe, making it a centre of railways and highways to the rest of Europe. Some major routes include, the TGV, with several trains daily from Paris, Avignon, Dijon, and Nice. Hourly trains to/from Milan with connections to all parts of Italy, and hourly ICE (German high-speed trains) from Zürich to Karlsruhe, Mannheim, Frankfurt in Germany, many continuing toward Amsterdam, Hamburg or Berlin.

The Swiss will spoil you with fantastic public transport - swift, punctual trains, clean buses, and a half dozen different kinds of mountain transport systems. In general there's at least one train or bus every hour.

Best time of year to visit

Switzerland offers a wide variety of things to do and see, whatever the season. Summer lasts roughly from June until September, and offers the most pleasant climate for outdoor activities. Temperatures average around 20°C to 25°C.

If you visit during the spring (April to May) or the autumn (September to October), you are likely to find fewer tourists and special promotions. Mountains and meadows are bursting with springtime wildflowers. Temperatures hover around 7°C to 14°C.

Winter sports venues begin operating in late-November and close down when the snow begins to melt in spring. However, really keen skiers can take to the slopes practically the whole year on a number of glaciers around the country. Temperatures drop to around 2°C to 6°C.

Switzerland has a variety of wacky and wonderful festivals that children and parents will love! May Day is dedicated entirely to children, and then there are the wild costumes of Silvesterkläuse and Vogel Gryff, as well as cow-fighting and whip-cracking competitions. The Interlaken Music Festival is one of the most important events on the Swiss classical music calendar. Performers at this annual summer spectacle always include leading international orchestras and soloists.

For eight colourful days at the end of January, the Alpine village of Château-d'Oex accommodates around 80 hot air balloons coming from 20 different countries. It is quite a spectacular sight.

February is carnival time in many towns with lively parades, musicians and elaborate costumes. During the carnival season, participants let their hair down and enjoy life to the fullest. Masks and costumes help people take on a new identity while they parade through the streets. Carnival is held throughout Switzerland, but the dates and details vary from canton to canton. It is normally just before or just after the beginning of Lent. Carnival is best known in Basel, but it's also lively in Zürich, Lucerne and Fribourg.

? Must know before you go

Closed on Sundays. Swiss employment law bans working on Sundays, so all shops stay closed. An exception is any business in a railway station, which is deemed to be serving travellers and so is exempt. If you want to find an open shop on a Sunday, go to the nearest railway station. If a business is family-owned, you aren't strictly employing anybody so you can open, hence small shops are often open on Sundays.

It is not part of the EU. Switzerland is not a member of the EU, however. Therefore, travellers entering Switzerland are subject to customs controls even if there are no immigration controls, and persons travelling elsewhere in the Schengen Area will also have to clear customs.

Discounts. Switzerland is certainly not a cheap place to travel. But there are discounts. Almost nobody in Switzerland pays full fare for the transit system. At the very least they all have a Half-Fare Card which saves you 50% on all national buses and trains and gives a discount on local and private transit systems. Annual half fare cards cost CHF165; visitors from abroad can buy a 1-month Half-Fare Card cards for CHF99. Children between ages 6 and 16 pay half price for travel around Switzerland.

🖼 Highlights

Ski in Style. Take to the slopes in Verbier and experience the very best in European skiing.

Historical Horse Race. Experience 'White Turf', a prestigious and traditional horse race event since 1907 or take the family to the famous Heidi Museum.

Train Travel in Style. This is as scenic as it gets – a train journey to the top of Europe, the Jungfrau rail is a once in a life time experience. The long train ride (about 2 hours each way) is a great opportunity to view Swiss villages up close.

Chocolates & Scenery. Spend half a day on a boat trip on Lake Zürich, before heading to the world famous 'Lindt' chocolate shop.

FUN FAMILY FACT:
The average Swiss eats 23lbs of chocolate per year compared to the 11.7lbs consumed by Americans; and Switzerland has the highest consumption of soft drinks in the world.

 Tip for the Trip

"If you want to ensure your little ones sleep well at night then take some portable black out blinds or cheaper still, some black bin liners and tape. They are easy to pack and you can stick them to the windows so you won't have to worry about light affecting the quality & consistency of your children's sleep."

Adventure:
Action + Adventure
Destination: Valais

IDEAL FOR
ALL
AGES

Switzerland

Whitepod Resort

Sion

The Lodge
Chez Dany Verbier

Haus Glacier
Zermatt

Swiss Chalet
& Findlehorf

France

Italy

✈ **Regional Information**

The Valais is exactly that: a long, narrow, L-shaped valley which was cut by glaciers between two alpine mountain ranges. The region has more high mountains than any other region in the Alps and is home to some of Europe's best ski resorts - Zermatt and Verbier. Naturally the region is popular in the winter months, but does also offer excellent summer outdoor activities for families too.

Zermatt is the most famous mountain town in Switzerland – largely because of the astonishing Matterhorn – probably the most recognisable and sought-after mountain shape in the world. Dominated by the mighty Matterhorn, this historic climbing town is both snow-sure and super-chic, combining an abundance of Alpine charm with discreet A-list appeal and the unmistakable heritage charm. Zermatt village dates back to the Middle Ages, and today ancient barns sit alongside tastefully modern hotels, while the car-free policy preserves the peace. Zermatt's three main ski areas are Sunnega, on the 'sunny side' of the valley, and the gateway to skiing at Unterrothorn (3,103 m), Stockhorn (3,405 m) and most famously, Gornergrat (3,100 m) which provides one of the greatest panoramic views anywhere, including Monte Rosa, at 4,634 m second in the Alps only to Mont Blanc in altitude and the Klein Matterhorn, reached by Europe's highest cable car. Furi, at the far end of the village, is the gateway to the Trockener Steg link to Klein Matterhorn and Theodulpass, close to the Italian border, and Schwarzsee, near the foot of the Matterhorn. Zermatt's does offer challenging bump runs but intermediates are also catered for here. If you are travelling with little ones too young to ski, then there are excellent childcare facilities and activities for families on and off the slopes, a good range of restaurants and children aged under 10 ski free – one of the most generous deals in world skiing. For those people who are not skiers or who decide to take the day off, the most appealing and available activity is the 18 mile (30 kilometre) trail system that snakes through the lower section of the mountain.

Adventure: Action + Adventure
Destination: Valais

These trails can be used for either snow hiking or snowshoeing. The trail system is within walking distance to the village and the trails go past some of the mountain huts, where a hiker can warm up, get something to eat, or meet up with a skier who is out on the mountain for the day. There are also a bunch of other activities available in the area, such as curling rinks in one hall, three ice rinks, and sleigh rides for younger children.

Finally, there is also an excellent nursery, Kinderparadies Zermatt, which accepts children from three months of age. The 300 square metre facility is located a 200 metres walk from the station and reservation is essential. Children aged four and older can join special kids classes in the ski schools.

Verbier has achieved a reputation as one of the great resorts of the world, attracting hard-core skiers from all over the world – but equally it is appealing for families. Lying in a wide sunny bowl above the Rhone Valley at the crossroads of Europe, Verbier has managed to retain plenty of Alpine charm to complement the razzle-dazzle cosmopolitan chic. Verbier's network of pistes is bolted on to a larger, four-valley system, its own slopes provide the most challenging skiing. Intermediates thrive here as well as advanced skiers and boarders, particularly on the network of lifts around Attelas, Ruinettes and Lac de Vaux. Bump skiers are tested on such arduous descents as Gentianes down to Tortin, or from the top of the Mont-Fort glacier which, at 3,330 m is the highest point, providing truly spectacular views across countless peaks, including the Matterhorn and Mont Blanc.

For those who don't want to ski then sit back and admire the mountains from the sky. There are mountain guide and local flight companies that offer panoramic flights via helicopter (weather depending) over the mountains and glaciers. Skiers, snowboarders and telemarkers can also take a helicopter ride into the very heart of the Swiss Alps and enjoy an original and challenging descent on one of Verbier's fantastic slopes. Under the supervision of a qualified guide and with pair of wide skis, these trips become accessible to everyone. Don't get too despondent if you don't go when planned though as helicopter travel is dictated largely by the weather. Finally, walking, hiking, or snowshoe with the family is usually on the high list of priorities for many. Cherries Walks offer private, tailor-made trips with a certified mountain guide and children can participate as long as they can walk a good distance.

The ski season for both resorts generally last from mid-December to late March. At higher altitudes, however, it is possible to ski into summer or even year-round on some glaciers. Although high altitude expeditions are not generally recommended for young children.

Places to Stay

Whitepod Resort

Whitepod, located in the village of Les Cerniers is an eco-resort in the truest sense of the term. Each year Whitepod builds wooden platforms upon a geodesic-dome 'pod' (that's akin to a smaller 'yurt' tent). The pods have no plumbing and no electricity. But they do have oil lamps and a fireplace that keeps the pod toasty warm. Each pod also has a full bed and stellar south-facing views of Mount Blanc.

Guide Price: from £282 per POD per night
Best Room: All rooms offer space and stunning views

VIP Ski Chalet Haus Glacier

A rather smart private lift takes you from the high street up to the exclusive Haus Glacier in Zermatt. The apartment sleeps six in understated elegance, with a large comfortable lounge and smart bedrooms with designer bathrooms. There are wrap-around balconies for both sunrise coffee and a relaxing drink as the sun goes down after a hard day on the hill

Guide Price: From £929 per week person based on 2 sharing inc flights from UK
Best Room: Double bedroom with balcony and has space for cot bed

The Lodge Virgin Limited Edition

Sir Richard Branson's stunning mountain retreat in Verbier, perched high in the Swiss Alps, is the perfect year-round family holiday. Complete with nine bedrooms and suites, an indoor pool, Jacuzzis and a friendly team of experienced staff. The ultimate in luxury for families.

Guide Price: From £2,890 per room for a 3 night stay, including all your meals and drinks
Best Room: The 'bunk' room sleeps 6 kids, with Xbox, plasma and beanbags

Places to Eat

Swiss Chalet, Zermatt

This Swiss speciality restaurant at the foot of the Matterhorn, is a great place for traditional Swiss fondue and raclette cheese specialities. Specialities include various cheese fondues, meat fondues, potato rösti specials and chocolate-fondue.

Findlerhof, Zermatt

This mountain restaurant is ideal for long lunches. It's perched in tiny Findeln, between the Sunnegga and Blauherd ski areas; the Matterhorn views are astonishing. The owners tend their own Alpine garden to provide lettuce for their salads and berries for vinaigrettes and hot desserts.

Chez Dany, Verbier

For fine dining on the slopes, restaurants don't come much better than Chez Dany. Located just above Verbier, the terrace has unsurpassed views of the valley below, while the menu is varied and delicious. It is consistently rated highly by 'foodies' and has a trendy, hip following.

Adventure: History + Culture
Destination: St. Moritz

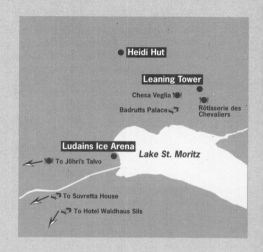

✈ Regional Information

St. Moritz, located in the Engadin region, is one of Switzerland's richest towns and certainly celebrated for its glitzy appeal. It became a world famous ski resort, after it has hosted two winter Olympic Games (1928, 1948), and is equally a popular family destination due to its 322 days year sunshine. St. Moritz has plenty to offer families who are looking for a spot of Swiss history and culture, not withstanding both summer and winter outdoor activities at a slow pace, which makes it ideal for a young family.

St. Moritz is home to 'Heidi's Hut'. Heidi was a well-known children's story about a little Swiss orphaned girl who was sent to live with her grumpy grandfather in the Alps. The film, which was set in Engadin, is one of the most famous attractions in the area. Children will enjoy this experience, especially if they have seen the film beforehand. The 'hut' can also be visited as part of the Heidi's Flower trail. The 1 kilometre long theme trail from Chantarella down to St. Moritz features around 200 species of plants, mainly protected alpines, which are laid out in attractive islands of flowers. A brochure, available free of charge from the Tourist Information, provides all the necessary information, and the spectacular scenery, with its forests of Swiss stone pine and varied flora, is a fitting backdrop. The trail is also suitable for all-terrain pushchairs, and young legs.

Being a sunny destination, St. Moritz (and its surrounding area) offers plenty of bathing. In the summer, even the mountain lakes warm up to a pleasant 20°C. Lej Marsch, one of the most popular bathing lakes in the region thanks to its sheltered yet sunny position and its proximity to the car park of the Olympic ski jump. Lake Staz, located between St Moritz and Pontresina, is perfect for water babies too. While the cooler Lake Cavloccio is a good one-hour hike from Maloja, the golf lakes on the banks of the River Inn are just around the corner. Well equipped with picnic areas, barbecue sites and children's playground, they are particularly ideal for families.

Adventure: History + Culture
Destination: St. Moritz

Families travelling in the summertime, looking for chilled activities can also ice-skate. There is an artificial ice-rink in Ludains Ice Arena in St. Moritz that is open from mid-July to mid-April. During winter months (approx. mid-December to end of February), ice sports can also be played on the additionally prepared natural ice rink. Rental of sport equipment and instruction is available on the spot, and children can generally participate from age 4 upwards.

Equally an interesting time to visit St. Moritz is in the Spring, especially for the Chalandamarz children's spring festival which features costumed parades. March 1st, is the day that children from the Engadin Valley chase away winter by singing and ringing cowbells. The local children don blue shirts and red caps and process through their towns carrying large bells, collecting treats and making a huge racket. Chalandamarz gained much publicity following the publication of the children's book Schellenursli, 'A Bell for Ursli', written by Selina Chönz and illustrated by Alois Carigiet. Look for this book if you ever go to the Engadin, as it's a fun gift and a wonderful keepsake.

Children will also love the many 'horse' experiences that St. Moritz has to offer. The Engadin region has some superb horseback riding for older children and the best stables are based in St. Moritz. Younger children can spend a few hours on a horse-drawn carriage, which can be also experienced on the frozen lake in the winter. The famous 'White Turf', which is a horse race held on the frozen lake in February, is also bit of fun for the family. Travellers arrive from all over the world flock to see the fine thoroughbreds take part in the races. On three Sundays in February, more than 30,000 spectators flock to the frozen expanse of the Lake of St. Moritz to witness the excitement and entertainment of the races against the magnificent backdrop of the mountains of the Engadin. This top winter event does not only appeal to enthusiastic horse lovers, but also offers a highly attractive fringe program. Included are three different art exhibitions, two interesting musical performances and a rich selection of culinary highlights.

Places to Stay

Hotel Waldhaus Sils
Located 7 miles from St. Moritz, the position of this hotel in a forest above a village is magical. This is not one of those 'kids' hotels where you are surrounded by animation - it is all very low-key. The atmosphere is friendly and the food is excellent. The details here are handled with care and everything runs smoothly, which is why the same families love to come back year after year.
Guide Price: From £260 prpn
Best Room: Family combination of a standard double room for the parents, smaller room for the children, two bathrooms, 50-57m²

Suvretta House
Since 1912, this upperclass mountain hideaway has offered a taste of the high life. A luxury fairytale castle, stylish and sophisticated for adults, yet child friendly at the same time. Rooms and suites are luxuriously decorated and spacious from Economy and Standard rooms, all the way to the Privacy Suite 544. They have a 'Teddy Club' restaurant for children and free Kindergarten in mornings and evenings
Guide Price: From £350 prpn
Best Room: Junior suite with separate shower and wet room

Badrutts Palace
One of Switzerland's landmark luxury hotels with fabulous mountain views, and very child-friendly. Kids will enjoy the Heidi House - a supervised play area with activities and movies, and parents will love the 'Palace Wellness' spa. There is special attention paid to families with a kid's welcome gift.
Guide Price: From £350 prpn
Best Room: Superior room with views of St. Moritz village

Places to Eat

Chesa Veglia, St. Moritz
Dating from 1658, it is one of the oldest farmhouses in St. Moritz. Now it houses three restaurants and two bars. The grill Chadafö provides the perfect setting for elegant dining with classic French cuisine. The two bars – the Polo Bar and Carigiet – are the perfect places to enjoy pre and after-dinner drinks and are ideally suited for families.

Rôtisserie des Chevaliers, St. Moritz
This exquisitely panelled grillroom, in one of the most historic hotels in St. Moritz, offers a cosy ambience that's especially suited to cold weather. Dishes are most often based on the freshest and best produce available in any given season.

Jöhri's Talvo, St. Moritz
Set in an Engadin house which dates back to the middle of the 17th century this restaurant was opened in 1992. It is located 10 minutes to the west of St Moritz in the suburb of Champfer and offers French and some regional Engadin cuisine.

Adventure:
Action + Adventure
Destination:
Interlaken & Jungfrau

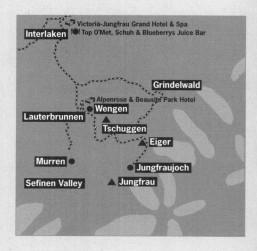

7 - 11 JUNIOR   **12 - 16** TEEN

✦ Regional Information

Interlaken is situated on the Aare River between the Brienz and Thun lakes, in the Bernese Oberland region at the foot of the three world famous mountains Eiger, Moench and Jungfrau. Thanks to its location and infrastructure Interlaken is the ideal base to stay for excursions to surrounding areas. The Interlaken region is a mecca for visitors who never have enough of spectacular scenery. By funicular and aerial cable way, families can take countless trips to the wonderful world of the Swiss Alps. You can follow in the footsteps of secret agent James Bond up to the Schilthorn with its famous Piz Gloria revolving restaurant and enjoy the views of more than 200 peaks.

The St. Beatus-Höhlen caves are situated at 6 kilometres (4 miles) from Interlaken, at the northern slope which borders the Thunersee. These stalactitic caves can be reached by car, but you can also take the boat or bus from Interlaken or Thun. The famous dripstone caves are located on the historic Pilgrims' Path, and can be reached by public transport or on foot. The site also features a Cave Museum providing an insight into the history and development of cave exploration in Switzerland. The wide variety of exhibits offer a fascinating glimpse into this magical underground world. A guided tour enables you to take a look inside the interior of the mountain world. The guide will give explanations, and you will have time to look around. Visiting the caves is not to be recommended if you are not a good walker or for small children.

The Jungfrau is one of the main summits in the Bernese Alps, situated between the cantons of Valais and Bern in Switzerland. Together with the Eiger and Mönch, the Jungfrau forms a massive wall overlooking the Bernese Oberland and is considered one of the most emblematic and most visited sights of the Swiss Alps.

Switzerland

Adventure: Action + Adventure
Destination: Interlaken & Jungfrau

Families seeking an adrenalin kick will find an array things to do in the Jungfrau Region. Zoom through the air at 80 km/h on the First Flyer. Feel the wind in your face on a scooter-bike, which you can hire at the First aerial cableway, and there is the Jungfraujoch - Top of Europe which has a fun park where you can slide down the snow slope in a variety of ways.

The construction of the Jungfraujoch railway in the early 20th century made the area one of the most-visited places in the Alps. Along with the Aletsch Glacier to the south, the Jungfrau is part of the Jungfrau-Aletsch Protected Area, which was declared a UNESCO World Heritage Site in 2001.

A visit to the Jungfraujoch, is really a must for any family. The Jungfraujoch is the highest situated train station in Europe at 3,454 m (11,332 ft) over sea. It has been in use since 1912. The plan to extend the railway to the summit of the Jungfrau is as old as the railway itself, but it remains a plan for the time being. A train leaves from Kleine Scheidegg; it mostly runs through a tunnel in the north face of the Eiger. In this tunnel the train will make a short stop at the station Eigerwand (2866 m, 9,403 ft), where you can get off for a short period of time to look down through windows in the north face of the Eiger. The next short stop is the station Eismeer (3,160 m, 10,366 ft). You will have the opportunity to enjoy the view on a world of ice. When you have arrived at the Jungfraujoch you can enjoy a breathtaking view over the Bernese Oberland on the one hand, and the Konkordiaplatz on the other hand. The Konkordiaplatz is an intersection of several glaciers, among which the Grosser Aletsch-glacier. Families can purchase a 'family card' for the whole brood, making it more affordable. Attractions at the top include the famous Eispalast (Ice Palace), and there are lofty alpine restaurants as well. Later you can take the family on a sleigh ride pulled by huskies, ride on a snowboard or ski.

Walking and hiking are equally popular activities for summer and winter months. The Jungfrau Eiger Walk is a well-built hiking trail, and is suitable for all ages of families. The walk is in a magnificent mountain setting and can be made from the Eigergletscher station to Kleine Scheidegg or in the opposite direction. The theme of the Jungfrau Eiger Walk is the Eiger North Wall with its decades of dramatic history – tales of triumph and tragedy. The walk takes about 50 minutes uphill and about 40 minutes downhill.

For older children, who love a challenge, there is glacier hiking available in the winter months. The two-day hike along the Aletsch glacier is an authentic adventure. An experienced mountain guide leads the participants through a glacier world that is as bizarre as it is fascinating. The high-Alpine hike leads from the Jungfraujoch over the longest ice stream in the Alps to the Märjelensee lake and on to Kühboden in Lötschental in the Valais. An overnight stop is made at the SAC Konkordia Hut, where hikers will enjoy cosy sleeping accommodation after a tasty cheese fondue.

Places to Stay

Alpenrose

In a tranquil position with stunning views and around 5 minutes from the station you will find the oldest hotel in Wengen, built at the end of the 19th century and Paul von Allmen's family have run the hotel ever since. The lounges and dining rooms are cosily decorated and have been recently remodelled in the beautiful Alpine style using old wood.

Best Room: Larger, superior rooms with bath, seating area and balcony with south western aspect
Guide Price: From £110 prpn

Beausite Park Hotel

A 40 room retreat set in beautiful gardens which also boasts an organic swimming pond. Dine on five-course meals and à la carte cuisine in the restaurant over panoramic views. Approximately ten minutes uphill walk from the main street and Wengen station.

Best Room: Junior suites have a separate sitting area and a balcony, and can accommodate a family of four
Guide Price: From £120 prpn

Victoria-Jungfrau Grand Hotel & Spa

One of Switzerland's best known classic yet historic spa hotels. All rooms have a distinctive design and décor, ranging from classic to contemporary and with views extending to the Jungfrau. Offers free accommodation for children up to 15, babysitting, Sony Playstation and games.

Best Room: Those facing south, for views of the snowcapped Jungfrau
Guide Price: From £265 prpn

Places to Eat

Top O'Met, Interlaken

Restaurant Top o'Met on the 16th floor of hotel Metropole offers a magnificent view of the town and the Jungfrau. You can eat indoors or on the terrace, while watching the activities of the paragliders. They may pass by at virtually no distance from the terrace on their way to the landing place across the street. The restaurant is not the cheapest one in town, but the excellent food and the view make it a great experience that can be highly recommended.

Schuh, Interlaken

Overlooking the world famous Jungfrau, Schuh is located in the heart of Interlaken. An institution since the beginning of the 19th century is deservedly known for its chocolates, many of which are unique concoctions. In the dining room try the veal schnitzel Zürich style.

Blueberrys Juice Bar, Interlaken

Located in the centre of Interlaken, and even though its a small snack bar, Blueberry's has phenomenal food. The food is either already prepared or fixed fresh within minutes of your order. Everything they sell is freshly made from scratch from juices, smoothies, muffins, cupcakes, bagels, wraps... great for hungry kids on the run.

Focus On...
Zürich

Zürich is rich in cultural highlights. With over 50 museums and more than 100 galleries, it is one of the world's major art trade centres. Zürich's cultural institutions such as the Opera House, the Tonhalle Orchestra, and the Schauspielhaus theatre tempt visitors and residents with high culture on the stage. Although Zürich may not be a first choice for families with teenagers (unless it is a stop over before spending some time on the slopes), it is a great city for families with smaller children.

The best and quickest way to see the city is to walk about the famous quays of Zürich, which are riverside promenades along the Limmat. Many of these quays open onto beautiful gardens where the entire family can rest their feet (there are also several outdoor play areas here, or you can pick up a map listing 80 different playgrounds at the tourist office). Or catch one of the regular ferry boats for a scenic 'round trip', which takes approximately 1.5 hours, with stops.

The town's major attraction is the Landesmuseum (Swiss National Museum), which has something for all ages, such as antique doll houses built over various periods for the very young. Boys in particular will be fascinated by the display of weapons and armour, and there are always special exhibitions. Families can also head for the Botanischer Garten, which features some 15,000 living specimens. If you've got some time to spare, you can visit either the Zürcher Spielzeugmuseum (Zürich Toy Museum) or one of the best zoos in Europe, Zoologischer Garten.

Winter time is when this city come alive. Every winter, there is an ice-skating rink in the courtyard of the Swiss National Museum to transform Zürich into a Christmas wonderland with a fabulous outdoor market to boot. Work up an appetite by climbing the 184 stairs in the Grossmunster, the towering church founded by Charlemagne: the city views will take your breath away. Then dine on soft macaroons, or warm up with hot chocolate from 'Confiserie Sprüngli'. The city is brimming with dining options, but a good spot for lunch is the lively, family friendly 'Café Terrasses' situated on the river, a place to be seen at the weekends. Children will love the cosy Swiss style fondue restaurant, 'Chaesalp', set up above the city. They have little rabbits, which children can sit and see through a glass screen, an outdoor patio for the summer.

The only place to stay in Zürich for families who want to experience authentic 'Swiss style' in luxury is the 'Dolder Grand'. Located on a hilltop 10 minutes outside of the city by car (or free Limo), the exquisite Dolder Grand is a haven of placid luxury for families seeking privacy and calm away from bustling Zürich. Originally built in 1899, the recently renovated property continues to boast a world-class spa and dining experience.

ⓘ Stylish Essentials

General Information

Tourist Information
www.myswitzerland.com
T. 00800 100 200 30
(UK Free phone)
E. info.uk@myswitzerland.com

Swiss Mountain Guide Association
www.4000plus.ch

Snow & Weather Reports
www.onthesnow.co.uk

Swiss Snow Sports
List of Schools
www.snowsports.ch
(German and French)
T. +41 (0)31 810 4111
for English enquiries.

Airlines

Swiss Airlines
www.swiss.com
T. +41 (0)848 700 700

Easyjet
www.easyjet.com
T. 0843 104 5000
(UK service centre)

BMI
www.flybmi.com
T. 0844 8484 888 (UK callers)
T. +44 (0)1332 64 8181
(International callers)

Rail/Boat Networks

TGV
www.tgv.co.uk

Rail Europe
www.raileurope.co.uk
T. 08448 484 064 (UK enquiries)

Swiss Travel Passes
www.swisstravelsystem.ch

Swiss Boat Pass
www.swissnavigation.ch

Festivals/ Events

Balloon Festival
Late January
Skies fill with colourful balloons
www.festivaldeballons.ch

Interlaken music festival
1st week of July
www.interlaken-classics.ch

St. Nicholas Day
6th December
Parades, Fairs celebrations

National Day
1st August
Fireworks, folk music, plays

White Turf
1st Half of February
St Moritz
International Horse Races
www.whiteturf.ch

Valais

Official Tourist Information
www.valais.ch
T. +41 (0)27 327 35 70
E. info@valais.ch

Cherries Walking Tours
Cherries Walks
T. +41 (0)79 239 2161
E. info@cherrieswalks.com

Ecole Suisse de Ski (ESS),
T. +41 (0)27 775 33 63
E. info@verbiersportplus.ch,

ES - European Snowsport
Verbier Ski School
T. +41 (0)27 771 6222,

Performance Verbier
Ski Centre, Verbier,
T. +41 (0)796 909 799

Whitetracks Helicopter
T. +41 (0)779 664 0841

Alpinemojo
T.+41 (0)764 642 521

Sleigh rides
T. +41 (0)79 436 76 12

Snow Kiting
Kite Rider GmbH, Chavezweg 5,
3911 Ried-Brig
T. +41 (0)78 628 59 73
www.snowkiting.ch

Whitepods
Les Cerniers
1871 Monthey, Switzerland
www.whitepod.com
T. +41 (0) 24 471 38 38

The Lodge
Verbier
www.thelodge.virgin.com
T. 0800 716 919 (UK enquiries)
E. enquiries@virginlimitededition.com

VIP Ski Lodge Haus Glacier
Zermatt
VIP SKI
www.vip-chalets.com
T. 0844 557 3119

Swiss Chalet
18 Bahnhofstrasse,
Zermatt
T. +41 (0)27 96 75 855

Chez Dany
Chemin de Clambin,
1936 Verbier
T. +41 (0)27 771 2524

Findlerhof
Findeln, Valais, CH-3920
Zermatt
T. +41 (0)27 9672588

St. Moritz

General Tourist Information
Via San Gian 30
CH-7500 St. Moritz
www.engadin.stmoritz.ch
E. allegra@estm.ch

Official Tourism
www.stmoritz.ch

White Turf
St. Moritz
www.whiteturf.ch

Badrutts Palace
Via Serlas 27
7500 St. Moritz
www.badruttspalace.com
T. +41 (0)81 837 1000
E. reservations@badruttspalace.com

Waldhaus Sils
CH-7514 Sils-Maria
www.waldhaus-sils.ch
T. +41 (0) 81 838 5100
E. mail@waldhaus-sils.cj

Hotel Suvretta House
Via Chasellas 1
CH - 7500 St. Moritz, Switzerland
www.suvrettahouse.ch
T. +41 (0)818 36 36 36
E. info@suvrettahouse.ch

Schloss Hotel Chaste
www.schlosshoteltarasp.ch
T. +41 (0)81 861 30 60

Chesa Veglia
www.badruttspalace.com
T. +41 (0)81 837 28 00

Rôtisserie des Chevaliers
Hotel Kulm, St Moritz
www.kulmhotel-stmoritz.ch
T. +41 (0)81 836 80 00

Jöhri's Talvo
Via Gunels 15
CH-7512 St Moritz-Champfer
www.talvo.ch

Jungfrau

Junfrau Tourist Information
www.jungfrau.ch

Grindlewald Sports
www.grindelwaldsports.ch
T. +41 (0)33 854 12 80
E. info@grindelwaldsports.ch

St. Beatus Caves
Beatus Höhlen 1
3800, Switzerland
www.beatushoehlen.ch
T. +41 (0)33 841 16 43

Top o'Met
Höheweg 37
CH-3800 Interlaken
www.metropole-interlaken.ch

Zürich

Landesmuseum
(Swiss National Museum)
Museumstrasse 2
8001 Zürich, Switzerland
www.musee-suisse.ch
T. +41 (0)44 218 65 11

Zoologischer Garten
Zürichbergstrasse 221
8044 Zürich, Switzerland
www.zoo.ch
T. +41 (0)44 254 25 00

Zürcher Spielzeugmuseum
(Zürich Toy Museum)
Fortunagasse 15
8001 Zürich, Switzerland
www.zuercher-spielzeugmuseum.ch
T. +41 (0)44 211 93 05

Café Les Terasses
Hönggerstrasse 115
8037 Zürich
www.cafe-terrasse.ch

Confiserie Sprüngli
www.spruengli.ch

Chaesalp
Toblehofstrasse 236
Zürich 8044
www.chaesalp.ch
T. +41 (0)44 260 7575

Dolder Grand
Kurhausstrasse 65
8032 Zürich, Switzerland
www.thedoldergrand.com
T. +44 (0)44 456 6000

Mellieha Festival with church view,
© Malta Tourism Authority, www.viewingmalta.com

MALTA & GOZO

St. Julians, Sliema & Valletta | Central Malta |
Gozo | Mellieha

MALTA & GOZO

Malta is an eclectic mix of North African and Arabic influence, Baroque architecture, and Sicilian-inspired cuisine and culture. It may not be an obvious first choice for families looking for a travel adventure, yet the year-round good weather and value for money, makes it particularly a good choice for young families or first time travellers. Malta, like most Mediterranean cultures, is very child friendly and offers an incredible variety of historical sites, golden beaches and fun festivals. For many families, piling children onto aeroplanes and keeping them entertained on a long haul is not a great way to start a trip, but, at only a two or three hour hop from most European countries, the island is near enough for the journey to be manageable.

There is no known area in the world the size of Malta that packs in so many ancient sites and splendid archaeological sites. The three small islands (Malta, Gozo and Comino), with a total land area of little more than 300 square kilometres embraces Neolithic temples older than the Pyramids; grand palaces built by the Knights of St John; great fortresses where history was made; a medieval walled city, and Baroque parish churches. At the very dawn of civilization, it was the Maltese who led the way, building massive, megalithic temples, which are now regarded as the oldest, free-standing buildings in the world. Malta has served as a watch keeper and guardian of the Mediterranean trade routes, which has been a launch-pad for European invaders and an idyllic retreat for rich aristocracy. Its history is long and complicated and its geography unique, and together these have made it one of the most enticing islands in Europe.

Naturally Malta has plenty of safe sandy beaches to spend days digging, making sandcastles, splashing in the sea and pretty harbours for evening strolls. The best beaches for families can be found in the North at Mellieha Bay or Golden Bay to the west, for a thrilling boat trip away there is Santa Maija Bay on Comino or spend a day at the ochre coloured sandy beach of Ramla Bay on Gozo.

But Malta offers much more than just the beach to keep youngsters busy. Depending on their age much of the history, culture and architecture of Valletta will no doubt be lost on many young visitors but the capital does have a few tricks up its sleeve to draw them in. The Great Siege of Malta, a special-effects historical show, guides them through a series of videos, tableaux's, touch-screens and various other special effects all geared at introducing young people to Valletta and the history of the 1565 Siege. Mdina (Malta's old walled city) is equally fascinating and young ones will enjoy taking a horse-drawn carriage around the narrow streets, delving into the historic past.

Gozo is equally, if not more impressive than Malta. It is home to man's comprehensive temple-building spree, the Ggantiji temples, the oldest freestanding structure on earth, and the Hypogeum containing a staggering 3600-year-old bones amongst others, and then there are plenty of sailing, snorkelling, diving and boat trips to enjoy the islands scenery and underwater world.

Festivals are plentiful. With carnivals, festas and music festivals continually occurring during the summer months, which make Malta appealing at that time of year – and also coincides with summer holidays. The variety of accommodation is equally impressive, from small family run farmhouses, to boutique hotel gems, families will definitely find something suitable for their budget.

🚌 Fun Facts

Capital: Valletta (Malta), Victoria (Gozo).

Population: 408,333.

Currency: Euro

Languages: Maltese and English.

Trivia: The earliest evidence of human habitation in Malta was found in the Ghar Dalem Cave, and the Temple at Ggantija on Gozo which predates the Egyptian pyramids.

✈ Getting there and exploring around

Europe is a smaller place thanks to the large number of budget airlines that have sprung up over recent years and the increase in airline competition is great news for anyone looking for flights to Malta. Malta was once a fairly expensive to get to and consequently lost out to much cheaper European destinations, but flights are now more reasonable.

Direct flights operate from most countries in mainland Europe. Major airlines with services to the island include KLM, Lufthansa and Swissair, but Malta's national airline Air Malta dominates the flight market. In contrast to the others, Air Malta operates direct flights to cities south of the island as well as north, and on to other destinations such as Istanbul.

Remember, if you are travelling with young children you may not be asked to pay the full price of a seat, depending on the airline you fly with. Often, if the child is under 2 years old, they will not be allocated a seat and instead required to sit on an adults lap and use a special seat belt provided by the airline.

Gozo has its own helicopter based at Xewkija from where it operates flights to Malta's airport in Luqa. Helicopter flights are a 10 minute luxury and certainly expensive compared to the alternative 20 minute ferry option. But for a special view of Malta and a flight to remember, consider it an investment.

Families can also arrive by sea, as Malta has regular sea links with Italy and Tunis. Virtu Ferries runs fast catamaran services to and from Sicily and Grimaldi ferries operates a service from Salerno, calling at Tunis.

Getting around Malta is fairly simple – taxis are cheap and are the best option. However if you are travelling distances it might be a better option to hire a private taxi company (such as NCks) who offer reasonable services and also have a range of child seats for safe travelling.

☼ Best time of year to visit

The weather in Malta is distinctly Mediterranean in feel. Similar to the other Mediterranean isles, its weather patterns are heavily influenced by the sea, with summers that are long, hot and dry. Temperatures during the summer months easily reach 30°C when the hot sirocco winds blow across the sea from North Africa. The winter months are generally milder, with temperatures rarely falling below 15 degrees and still maintain 5 or 6 hours of sunshine per day. Occasionally colder winds blow south or southeast from central Europe, which can bring with it chillier spells, but these tend to be short lived. The Maltese justifiably have a lot to celebrate, and local festivals, similar to those in southern Italy, are commonplace in Malta and Gozo. Festivals and religious events abound on the island and you won't have to look far to witness some kind of festivity.

The annual Carnival takes place on the week leading up to Ash Wednesday and has had an important place on the cultural calendar. It typically includes masked balls, fancy dress and grotesque mask competitions, lavish late-night parties, a colourful, parades of floats with marching bands and costumed revellers.

L'Imnarja - the festival of St Peter and St Paul - is also one of the most popular summer festivals and is celebrated by thousands. It takes place at the end of June, the streets come alive with colourful music and dancing, families picnic around the clock in the Buskett Gardens.

Festas are held throughout the summer months between May and September in honour of the patron saints of various villages. Parades with brass bands and elaborately costumed villagers celebrate the saint's feast day with confetti, nougat, and displays Malta's legendary fireworks.

? Must know before you go

Driving. Malta has the highest road accidents in Europe – Maltese drivers don't believe in speed restrictions. If you have to get behind the wheel the heed caution, remember they also drive on the left like the British.

Steps and pavements. For small children and pushchairs, certain parts of Malta can be difficult to get around. The narrow streets and pavements can almost be impossible to walk on without nearly getting hit by a passing car. Take caution with toddlers, especially as there are many uneven pavements and lots of steps to negotiate (particularly in the historical areas like Mdina).

Food and drink. You'll be amazed and stunned by the quality of fresh fruit and vegetables. The best (and freshest) are sold by hawkers at the side of the road. Beware of hawkers that go around the more touristic villages as some are known to overcharge tourists unfortunately. Tap water, although often advised otherwise, is safe to drink but the taste isn't spectacular to say the least. To be on the safe side offer children bottled water.

Highlights

Spinola Bay. A walk around pretty Spinola Bay in the early evening and as the sun sets, dine at one of the smart restaurants overlooking the bay.

Mdina Magic. Take a horse drawn carriage around the walled city of Mdina and stop for afternoon tea at the Fontenalla Gardens.

Gozo by Sea. Visit Dwejra point and the gigantic caves, and snorkel or scuba dive on the blue lagoon on Comino.

Mellieha Beaches. Spend a day digging and making sandcastles on the family friendly Mellieha Bay.

FUN FAMiLY FACT:
Wondering why Malta has such an affinity with nearby Italian island Sicily? Before the Ice Age there used to be a land bridge connecting the two islands.

 Tip for the Trip

"If this is your first trip with your children, plan for a slower pace than you might usually attempt. If you want to see more than one place, be realistic about what you can cover with little ones in tow. Plan for naps, frequent meals, toilet/nappy stops and also times of the day when they can just sit and play."

Adventure: Reflect + Re-new
Destination:
St. Julians, Sliema & Valletta

IDEAL FOR
ALL
AGES

● Casino

Mediterranean Sea

Hotel George

Hilton Malta

Spinola
Peppino's
Terrazza
Hotel Juliana
St. Julian's

● St. Julians Tower

Mint Café
● Il-Fortizza
Sliema

To Valletta

Tigne Fort

Manoel Island

+ Regional Information

Malta might have been recognised as a 'package holiday' type destination in the past. But all that has changed. The upmarket and picturesque villages of St. Julians and Spinola Bay, although still brimming with tourists, are equally popular with locals and are a great base to stay and explore the eastern side of Malta and its surrounding coastline. Staying in this part of Malta can be a pleasantly calm (and yes, relaxing) family trip.

Sliema and St Julian's are Malta's main coastal resort towns and a heartland for shopping, entertainment and café life. Nearby 'Paceville' is Malta's main nightlife area (NB not a great place for sleeping children and families who want peace and quiet!). Bay Street is a colourful, vibrant shopping complex, located in the centre of St. Julians, and has pretty much everything you could want. It is a shaded haven for pram pushers and a great place to shop for games, clothes and toys for children. A stroll around St. Julians harbour (marvelling at the super yachts) in the evening makes a pleasant activity.

Spinola Bay (which is an extended part of St. Julians) has a sprawl of excellent restaurants and cafes. In the summer months there is often some form of street entertainment, such as bands, and markets which are operated by local farmers. A stroll around this area of an evening is a must.

A short bus or boat ride away is Valletta, the capital of Malta. The name 'Valletta' is traditionally reserved for the historic walled citadel that serves as Malta's principal administrative district. It is a stunning city (which is currently being modernised), yet contains buildings from the 16th century onwards. The city is essentially Baroque in character, with elements of Mannerist, Neo-Classical and Modern architecture in selected areas, though World War II left major scars on the city. The City of Valletta was officially recognised as a World Heritage Site by UNESCO in 1980. A day spent here is worthwhile, depending on the age of your children.

Adventure: Reflect + Re-new
Destination: St. Julians, Sliema & Valletta

The capital city of Valletta also hosts regular plays and concerts, as well as scores of exhibitions and street events. The Museum of Archaeology in Valletta has an exceptionally rich collection of prehistoric artefacts. The War Museum at Fort St. Elmo is home to a Sunday military parade in period costumes re-enactment and the capital also possesses the impressive Grand Master's Palace and St. John's Co-cathedral.

Probably most impressive to children will be the 'Upper Barrakka Gardens', which have panoramic views of the Grand Harbour. They were first constructed in 1661 for the private use of knights from Italy. It was not before 1824 that the gardens were opened to the public. The garden paths are lined with flowers, statues and plaques illustrating various personalities and significant events from Maltese history. Of special interest are the bronze group by Maltese sculptor Antonio Sciortino, entitled 'Les Gavroches'. Its depiction of three running children reflects those extreme hardships faced by the people of Malta at the turn of the 20th century. Finally children, may also enjoy the 'Malta Experience', which is an engaging audio visual spectacular about the 7,000 years of history in 45 minutes – the attraction offers stunning images projected onto a large panoramic screen with full sound affects, this will definitely keep children mesmerised.

For some light hearted 'family fun' then there are plenty of activities further afield, in Hal Far (south of Valletta), where lies 'Playmobil'. A fun, play park suitable for children aged 0-8 years, it follows the 'Legoland' theme of a 45 minute factory tour, free play areas and 'station's to make Playmobil characters. There is a good outdoor area with slides, sand pits and climbing frames for energetic children. Hera Cruises also offers plenty of boat trips departing from Sliema on board a luxury Turkish Gulet to nearby Comino, Gozo and other 'round trip' excursions around Malta.

One of the best ways to get acquainted with Malta by land, is by hopping on an open-top bus for a sightseeing tour. 'City Sightseeing Malta' operates red double-decker hop-on hop-off services with stops at the most important tourist attractions and visitor sites. Options include North Tour, South Tour and Tour of Gozo. All tours have a detailed multilingual audio commentary, and children will definitely find this engaging.

🔖 Places to Stay

Hotel Juliani

Malta's first boutique hotel is still the epitome of luxury contemporary style. It is situated in the centre of bustling Spinola Bay, and has a tiny rooftop pool with fabulous views of the harbour.

Guide Price: From £90 prpn
Best Room: 45m² Ambassador Suites with private balcony

Hotel George

Staff are welcoming at this super cool, hip hotel. It has been modernized to the highest standards, with a cute rooftop pool and some suites also have terraces and separate sitting areas which make it ideal for families. There is also a 'serve yourself' honesty bar next to reception with treats and snacks for young travellers. They offer excellent baby cots too, and roll-out beds for older children.

Guide Price: From £100 per suite per night
Best Room: Penthouse suites come with a choice of twin or queen size beds, sitting room and a 15m² terrace perfect for private sunbathing.

Hilton Malta

At the heart of the fashionable Portomaso waterfront, the hotel is 15 minutes' drive from Valletta, housing its own private marina and beach club. This is the place for families who want to be looked after. Although part of the global resort chain, this hotel does have some charm and is definitely one of the best options for families in Malta. They have a little beach and play area which young tots will love.

Guide Price: From £200 prpn
Best Room: Corner suite with sea views

🍽 Places to Eat

Peppino's, Spinola Bay

Set in the picturesque bay of Spinola Bay, Peppino's has become an institution in the food industry and is well known for its Italian and French cuisine. Try to bag a table next to the gaping window for the views of the bay. Good for early diners.

Mint Café, Sliema

Located on the waterfront, Mint isn't the typical cafe' one finds in Malta. The food and sweets offered are versatile and innovative from the pesto and feta cheese muffin to the Quinoa salad and the gorgeous Pavlovas. They also serve gluten free treats too. Children will love to be spoilt with the super range of home-baked cakes and you can sit outside on the terrace as there are huge umbrellas in the shade.

Terrazza Restaurant & Wine Bar, Spinola Bay

Sit high up on the terrace and marvel at the views. There is a substantial selection of Mediterranean dishes with an emphasis on the local, including lots of pastas (gluten-free varieties available), fresh fish (fried or in a salt crust) and Maltese specialities. There is also a Mini Man Menu for children too.

Adventure: History + Culture
Destination: Central Malta

3-6 PRE-SCHOOLER

7-11 JUNIOR

Fort Madliena

Palazzo Parisio

Mosta Dome

Bacchus & Fontanella Tea Gardens

Three Villages

Xara Palace   Mdina

San Anton Palace & Gardens

Parruccan   Rabat

Verdala Palace & Buskett Gardens

Dingli Cliffs

Clapham Junction Cart Tracks

Med Sea

✦ Regional Information

Malta has had such a rich history that the country is practically saturated with attractions and places of interest. Central Malta is dominated by Malta's ancient capital, Mdina, a near perfect example of a medieval walled town. Beyond the walls, lies Rabat, a large town of Roman origin, which was once part of Mdina. To the south lies the incredible Dingli Cliffs, which are a perfect spot for hiking and picnics, while the Verdala Palace and San Anton Palace are both stunning historical sites with pretty shaded gardens.

Mdina is Malta's most beautiful city and fondly know as the 'Silent city', yet it fills up with tourists during the day, but is quiet and subdued at night when the crowds depart. It and neighbouring Rabat, were once part of the same settlement, but the Arabs walled off Mdina and made it a fortress city. The city can be explored on foot as it is fairly compact, but for children it is more interesting to take one of the horse and carriage rides (which can be found at the main gate entrance). The trip will take you around the city in approximately 30 minutes, and the guide will point out interesting features such as the St. Pauls Cathedral, and stop at the Mdina experience (an audiovisual experience of the city's history). Just outside the main gates there is a small children play area, which is suitable for toddlers and juniors to run off some energy. Also outside the gates there is a mini-train called 'The Peprina' which takes passengers around Rabat and its nearby villages. In 30 minutes you'll cover an in-depth view of the historical areas (including nearby Rabat) and buildings dating back from the Phoenicians to the mediaeval era as well as the British colonisation period.

Rabat means 'suburb' in old Arabic and this is indeed because Rabat is the town lying outside the citadel. Rabat had walls of its own in Roman times but this can only be seen today in parts of the street pattern. Many of Malta's most deeply resonant religious sites are concentrated in Rabat, such as St. Paul's church, with St. Paul's grotto, where the saint apparently lived after being shipwrecked on his way to being put on trial in Rome. Pope John Paul II visited this place of pilgrimage in 1990.

Adventure: History + Culture
Destination: Central Malta

The Roman Museum which houses the remains of a Roman villa, features mosaics and sculpture from the original house excavated on the site, along with artefacts and displays relating the Roman, Byzantine and Arab periods, from the 3rd century B.C. through the 10th century A.D. Finally the catacombs of St. Paul and St. Agatha, are early Christian underground cemeteries, and are certainly interesting for older children to visit.

To the south of Malta and reachable by road within 30 minutes from Mdina, is the Dingli Cliffs. The cliffs are the most spectacular natural monuments in Malta and rank among the more impressive landmarks in the Mediterranean. The coastal road runs above the high cliffs and provides access to the most breathtaking views of the sea and the tiny island of Filfla, (the cliffs rise up an astounding 250 metres above sea level). Besides their natural beauty, the cliffs are home to a variety of wildlife and birds and the small town of Dingli, which is the gateway to some of the best coastal walks in Malta. The town itself has a number of small bars and restaurants – if you have an early start with little ones it will pay off, as the best time of the day is early morning sun or in the evening when the most fantastic sunsets can be seen from the cliffs.

Not far away from the cliffs are the Buskett Gardens and the Verdala Palace (the official residence of the president of Malta). Buskett Gardens is Malta's only large area of woodland which was originally planted by the Knights as a hunting ground. Buskett has vineyards, orangeries, olive and lemon groves, and is heavily wooded with native, hardy species such as Mediterranean pines. As well as tourists, Buskett Gardens is a favourite location for the locals (it gets busy at weekends) picnic tables are provided and shaded walks weave their way throughout the gardens. In June, on the feast of St Peter and St Paul (L'Imnarja), Buskett Gardens is the focal point of the lively folk festival with traditional rabbit stew and Maltese wine being served.

To the east of Mdina, between the cities of Attard and Lija, lies San Anton Palace and Gardens. The gardens were laid out by Grand Master Antoine de Paule as grounds to his summer residence, San Anton Palace. The garden is a botanical delight. You can wander among mature trees, past old stone urns, and formal flower beds. At the centre of the garden is a duck pond, with fountains and water lilies and a bird aviary. This is a wonderful and easy spot, especially for toddlers and babies.

The central region really has some of the most interesting inland options, ranging from palaces to town house hotels. A stay here, even for just a few nights, to explore the areas highlights would make an interesting and unique experience for families.

Place to Stay

Xara Palace Relais & Châteaux

The Xara Palace is Malta's only 5-star luxury boutique hotel hidden away in the medieval fortified city of Mdina. It is the only place to stay within the fortified city, and certainly doesn't disappoint. The exquisite welcoming and attention to detail is worlds away from the bustling resorts of the coast. The generous antique-filled rooms have quirky touches and the bar in the glass-roofed atrium used to be a church organ.

They also have a superb restaurant, with an outside terrace on the ground floor, which serves excellent Italian food (and traditional pizzas) and opens early doors for families. The Palace is an excellent choice for couples and romantics, so staying here might not be an obvious choice for families, however for a couple of nights, to use as a base for exploring the delights of central Malta, results in an exceptionally different experience for children and parents alike.

Guide Price: From £300 prpn
Best Room: Duplex rooms with high ceilings and separating sleeping and living quarters

Places to Eat

Bacchus Restaurant, Mdina

Bacchus is an exquisite restaurant within the fortifications of Mdina. The restaurant location is like stepping inside a vaulted cellar, and the building dates back to 1658 with outstanding architecture ranging from the Roman to the Medieval times. It serves delicious fine French and Mediterranean cuisine and suitable choices for children too.

Fontanella Tea Gardens, Mdina

These ivy-draped tea gardens perched high on the walls of Mdina, have spectacular views and serve delicious cakes and teas. A great spot for afternoon tea after visiting the city walls. It can get very busy with visiting tourists though, so try to arrive early or late in the day.

Parruccan, Rabat

Children will love this place. It is located on the main square in Rabat, and is a typical Maltese cakes & nougat stand. Everything is fresh and local, and the 'fig rolls' are especially sweet – a great place to quickly fill hungry tummies or to take-away to the nearby gardens for a picnic.

Adventure:
Action + Adventure
Destination: Gozo

IDEAL FOR
ALL
AGES

✦ Regional Information

Gozo operates at a much slower pace than neighbouring Malta. Yet, it's an exciting destination, and provides visitors with some of Europe's most compelling outdoor experiences, medieval architecture, pretty farmhouses and historical sites. Even reaching the island is an exciting adventure, especially for children. The ferry (which crosses frequently) from Malta, takes approximately 30 minutes and is really the only way to reach the island. Leaving the Northern-most point of Malta's Cirkewwa dock and passing by the quaint island of Comino to land in Mgarr harbour, is a fun and easy trip with children. Lastly, Gozo also possesses several lovely sandy beaches for young ones and some of the best dive sites in the Mediterranean for both novices and the experienced.

Nearly a quarter of the population of Gozo inhabit the capital Victoria, more commonly known as Rabat (not to be confused by Malta's Rabat) by the local inhabitants is the main commercial centre of the island. The rest live in the other villages that surround Victoria. Victoria itself is a lovely small town which possesses charm and character, with an abundance of shops and restaurants all centred on the main 'Independence Square'. There are numerous markets at weekends and during the summer months the square is home to a local orchestra which holds free outdoor concerts in the evenings. This is a must for any travellers, as the place come to life in the evenings as local families appearing with children after the sun sets.

The Citadel which dominates the capital and is the main tourist attraction of Gozo. This old fortified city hides behind its bastions a number of fine buildings, museums and the Cathedral Church. From the huge walls of the fortifications a breathtaking panorama unfolds, where all the villages with their dominant church domes can be seen. Situated in the heart of Victoria is the Basilica of St. George just off the open air market in Independence Square. The medieval narrow streets that surround this Basilica instil a feeling of times gone by and are worth a glimpse

TEATRU ASTRA

Adventure: Action + Adventure
Destination: Gozo

Surrounded by sea, naturally Gozo offers a wide range of water sports, such as paragliding, sailing and of course scuba diving. Over the past decade, scuba diving in Gozo has really grown in popularity. This is no surprise considering the many scenic dive sites that can be found around both Gozo and Comino. Scuba divers will encounter dive sites with beautifully coloured coral reefs, dark caves, such as Cathedral cave and Coral cave, which over the years have become the habitat for various species of fish and other marine life.

What makes Gozo so attractive for scuba diving is the unique topography, mild weather, relatively clean waters and rich marine life. In summer, the warm sea temperature (averaging 26°C) makes it possible for divers to wear a light 3mm diving suit, and thus easy for beginners (and children) to learn. There are a number of PADI certified scuba diving schools in Gozo who offer short beginner courses and for the youngest divers the 'bubblemaker' course. Course instructors will take beginning divers to the more shallow waters to teach them the basic techniques of diving. Later on, diving instructors will move to more interesting sites. The blue lagoon on Comino is a remote setting, which makes a great day trip by boat for the whole family. There is no beach there but families can enjoy the shallow child-friendly waters and the lagoon is a great spot for snorkelling.

Gozo is also an excellent place for mountain biking with its serene environment and breathtaking views. There are a couple of routes are easy to follow, and bikes can be hired through many local agencies. The Dwejra route is good for beginners in mountain biking. The highlight of the Dwejra route is the Azure window (a rocky opening framing stunning views) and fungus rock, the sheer cliffs, curving bays and gigantic caves. The Zebbug track requires an intermediate level of biking skill. The main highlights are Il-Qolla l-Bajda (which is a weird looking hill), Is-Salvatur (which is a statue of Jesus on a hill) and the picturesque Gozitan countryside.

Beaches in Gozo are plentiful. Probably one of the most popular for families is the golden sandy beach of Ramla Bay. Out of season it is much quieter and is like a corner of paradise, during the summer it can get crowded. But it is accessible from the road, has a little café and many street sellers enticing your children with buckets, spades and brightly coloured beach towels.

For culture vultures, Gozo has enough historical sites to fill an entire week. With 7,000 years of history, the Megalithic Temples Ggantija (the giant's tower) is the oldest freestanding temple in the world, and is not to be missed. Despite being quite exposed it has survived the elements quite well and its construction shows the ingenuity of the race that inhabited these islands. This may not appeal to very young children, but older children will love learning about the history of the temple. And there is the 'Astra Theatre' which offers a wide vista of culturally oriented activities in Gozo. Local talent is extensively featured and encouraged with special prominence to operas.

Places to Stay

Maria Giovanna Guest House

Maria Giovanna Guest House is located in Marsalforn Bay, a typical Maltese town house which has just been renovated. Typical Gozitan furnishings, modern design and comforts melt to create the peaceful atmosphere of a small hospitable B&B. Offering home cooked breakfasts and fantastic cakes.

Guide Price: From £100 prpn
Best Room: Room 10 which has a little balcony and views of the bay

Cornucopia Hotel

The 4 Star Cornocupia Hotel is located on the outskirts of the Gozitan village of Xaghra, set on a high ridge with views over the Imrik valley, stretching towards the capital city Victoria and down to the sea of the seaside village of Marsalforn. The Hotel was initially a large local farmhouse which has been tastefully converted into a 48 guest room hotel and 11 self catering bungalows.

Guide Price: From £100 per bungalow per night
Best Room: A family bungalow with private terrace and stunning views

Kempinski San Lawrenz

This is by far the best accommodation option in Gozo for families looking for a spot of luxury, yet it still retains some Gozitan charm. This elegant and rustic retreat has 122 well appointed rooms and an excellent children's pool and activity room. For parents, there is a world class Ayurvedic spa offering special massages and body wraps. Its location - within walking distance from a craft market and San Lawrenz village - is ideal for families wanting a quiet, relaxing stay.

Guide Price: From £300 per suite per night
Best Room: 2-bedroom family suite with a sitting area and pool and garden views.

Places to Eat

Tatitas, San Lawrenz

A bright, smart and relaxing restaurant in the square of San Lawrenz, with an outside terrace. Offering Maltese/Italian dishes including fish delivered daily by the fishermen landing at Dwejra on the coast nearby, and vegetables from the restaurant's own garden. There is also excellent homemade Gozitan ice cream

Maji Wine, Victoria

A real foodie find. This place is located in the centre of Victoria (near the square) and has stunning views from the open roof terrace. Blink and you'll miss the entrance, as it is small and unassuming. Although this restaurant is considered 'top end', and billed as a wine bar as well as restaurant, the atmosphere is very relaxed and families are welcome (there is even a small children's menu).

Jeffrey's, Gharb

A local favourite, serving up delicious and authentic local cuisine at bargain prices, both inside and in an outside courtyard. It's small, so pre-booking in the summer is a must. Also note that the toilets are tiny and there are no baby changing facilities.

Opposite page. Mellieha church.

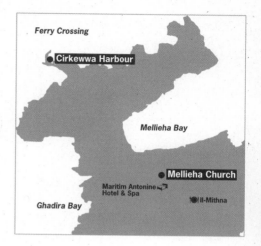

Focus On...
Mellieha

Mellieha is a rural village in the Northwestern part of Malta and derives its name from the Semitic root 'm-l-h' which in Arabic means salt. The name was probably derived from the ancient Punic and Roman salt-terns; historians indicated as lying adjacent to the large sandy bay at the foot of the village. Mellieha is one of Malta's most picturesque tourist destinations, and the town centre boasts a couple of fine restaurants and cute traditional shops. It's an ideal destination for families looking for a beach holiday and easy access for day trips to neighbouring Gozo and Comino.

Mellieha Bay is Malta's largest sandy beach and one of the best beaches in the whole of the Mediterranean. Ghadira Bay in Mellieha is very accessible, and has just a few steps and a ramped access down to the sand. Although it can get a little crowded especially during the months of June to September on the weekends. There are some very good facilities for bathers including snack bars and cafes. There are also water sports facilities where you can hire a pedalo, try parasailing or swim out to a large floating play area. It is very popular with families and there are many sun beds and umbrellas available for rent.

Families looking for a value for money, mid sized hotel will be well accommodated at 'The Maritim Antonine Hotel & Spa', which is situated in the centre of Mellieha village. Perched on a majestic spot on terraced hillsides with exquisite views of the church, the bay, the islands of Gozo and Comino, and the village, this gem may be part of a chain – but don't let that put you off. There are 3 little pools, (one on the roof terrace) and all rooms are modern, well appointed, and generous in size.

Il-Mithna means the windmill and this restaurant is in a 17th century mill built by the Knights of St John. The historic setting and al fresco dining is relaxed and informal – meaning great for families. The mainly serve Mediterranean and Maltese dishes major on meat for the main courses – including rabbit, the national meat of Malta – but also with seafood options.

Mellieha's main festive season occurs in the first two weeks of September and reaches its climax on the 8th September. During these days various cultural manifestations are held, such as musical concerts, fireworks, folk singing, art exhibitions and the traditional religious procession. A week stay in Mellieha can be relaxing and sufficient for a quiet family break.

ⓘ Stylish Essentials

General Information

Official Malta Tourism
www.visitmalta.com

Malta with children Guide
Information on things to do & when
www.maltababyandkids.com

Kids Malta
Online resource for classes,
courses and events
www.kidsmalta.com
E. info@kidsmalta.com

Malta Pass
Malta Pass Limited
Forni Terminal, Valletta Waterfront,
Pinto Wharf Floriana FRN 1913
www. maltapass.com.mt
T. +356 (0) 2744 2233

Airlines

Air Malta
Fly to Valletta from various locations.
www.airmalta.com

British Airways
From the UK, from Manchester
and London to Valletta.
www.ba.com

Virtu Ferries
www.virtuferries.com
T. +356 (0) 2122 8777

Grimaldi Ferries
www.grimaldi-ferries.com
T. +356 (0) 2122 6873

Gozo Channel Company
www.gozochannel.com
T. +356 (0) 2210 9000
(Timetable enquiries)

Ncks
24 Hour chauffeur services
www.nicks1.com
T. +356 (0) 7947 2131
E. info@nicks1.com

St Julians & Sliema

Bay Street Complex
St. Julian's
Malta
T. +356 (0) 2138 4422
E. info@baystreet.com.mt

Open Top Bus Tours
www.citysightseeingmalta.com
T. +356 (0) 2182 2415

Malta experience

St. Elmo Bastion,
Mediterranean St,
Valletta
www.maltaexperience.com
T. +356 (0) 2124 3776

Playmobil Funpark
HF80, Industrial Estate
Hal Far BBG3000 Malta
www.playmobil.com
T. +356 (0) 2224 2445
E. funpark@playmobilmalta.com

Hera Cruises
4 Abate Rigord st,
Ta'Xbiex XBX 1127
Malta
www.heracruises.com
T. +356 (0) 2133 0583
E. info@heracruises.com

Hilton Malta
Portomaso St Julians
Malta PTM 01, Malta
www.hilton.com
T. +356 (0) 2138 3383

Hotel Juliani
12 St. George's Rd
St. Julians STJ 3208 Malta
www.hoteljuliani.com
T. +356 (0) 2138 8000
E. info@hoteljuliani.com

The George Hotel
Triq Paceville Ave, Paceville
St Julian's STJ 3013, Malta
www.thegeorgehotelmalta.com
T. +356 (0) 2011 1000

Peppino's
31 St. Georges Road,
St. Julian,Spinola Bay,
Malta
www.peppinosmalta.com
T. +356 (0) 2137 3200

Mint Café
30/39 Luzio Junction/Stella Maris St,
Sliema,
SLM1599, Malta
www.mintmalta.com
T. +356 (0) 2133 7177

Terrazza Restaurant & wine bar
St Julian's
Malta
www.terrazza.eu
T. +356 (0) 2138 4939

Central Malta

Valletta Information
31, South Street,
VLT 11 31, South Street, Malta
www.cityofvalletta.org

The Malta Experience
Saint Elmo Bastions,
Mediterranean Street,
Valletta VLT06, Malta
www.themaltaexperience.com
T. +356 (0) 2124 3776

Xara Palace
Mdina,
MDN 1050 Malta
www.xarapalace.com.mt
T. +356 (0) 2145 0560

Bacchus Restaurant
Inguanez St, Mdina, Malta
T. +356 (0) 2145 4981
E. reservations@bacchus.com.mt

Fontenella Tea Gardens
1, Bastions Street, Mdina
www.fontanellateagarden.com

Gozo

Gozo Tourist Information
www.visitgozo.com

PADI Dive Centres
www.padi.com

Gozo Boat Trips
Status Quo,
Daleland Street,
Qala, Gozo.
www.barbarossa-excursions.com
E. info@barbarossa-excursions.com

Astra Theatre
Republic Street
Victoria
T. +356 (0) 2155 6256
E. lastella@vol.net.mt

Kempinski San Lawrenz
Triq ir-Rokon
San Lawrenz
Gozo
www.kempinski.com
T. +353 (0) 2211 5210

Cornucopia Hotel
10 Gnien Imrik Street,
Xaghra, Gozo,
www.cornucopiahotel.com
T. +353 (0) 2155 6486

Maria Giovanna Farmhouses
Rabat Road, Marsalforn, Gozo
www.gozoguesthouses.com
E. bugejajoe@vol.net.mt
T. +356 (0) 2155 3630

Jeffrey's
10 Gharb Road, Gharb, Gozo
www.jeffreysrestaurantgozo.com
T. +356 (0) 2156 1006

Tatitas Restaurant
San Lawrenz Square,
San Lawrenz, Gozo
T. +356 (0) 2156 6482
E. tatitas@malanet.net

Maji Wine
6 Sir Adrian Dingli Street
Victoria, Gozo
www.majiwine-dine.com
T. +356 (0) 2155 0878

Mellieha

Il-Mithna
58 Main Street, Mellieha
www.mithna.com
T. +356 (0) 2152 0404

Maritim Antonine Hotel & Spa
Borg Olivier St
Mellieha MLH 1021, Malta
www.maritim.com.mt
T. +356 (0) 2152 0923

Golden camels outside Royal Mirage Hotel

UNITED ARAB EMIRATES

Dubai | Abu Dhabi | Ras al-Khaimah | Hatta

UNITED ARAB EMIRATES ● ● ●

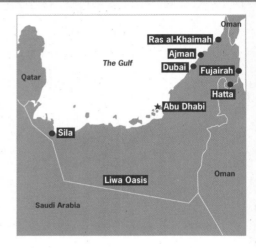

♛ Why is this place so special?

The United Arab Emirates is a constitutional federation of seven emirates; Abu Dhabi, Dubai, Sharjah, Ajman, Umm al-Qaiwain, Ras al-Khaimah and Fujairah. Four-fifths of the UAE is mainly desert, yet it is a country of contrasting landscapes, from awe-inspiring dunes to rich oases, precipitous rocky mountains to fertile plains, and not forgetting glitzy vibrant cities.

It is one of the world's fastest growing tourist destinations, and has all the right ingredients for an unforgettable family trip sun, sand, sea, sports, unbeatable shopping, top-class hotels and restaurants, an intriguing traditional culture, and a safe, welcoming environment.

Travel agencies and tour operators across the world have encouraged travellers to the UAE in their droves though the 'package holiday concept', however the area is still one of the best places in the Gulf for the independent traveller, offering a variety of unique 'Arabian' cultural experiences.

The emirates, though fairly small in size, each has their own unique features, and government systems. The capital, Abu Dhabi, is one of the world's most modern cities, while Dubai is undeniably one of the most vibrant cities in the Gulf. The Northern Emirates, such as Ras al-Khaimah and Ajman offer historical and cultural experiences in a much quieter, low-key setting, and further afield is the Al Hajar Mountain range, (which is the highest in Eastern Arabia) and nearby Hatta which can offer families a thrilling driving experience through dramatic canyons, deep gorges and rocky valleys.

The United Arab Emirates also has a diverse and multicultural society. Although the Emirati culture mainly revolves around the religion of Islam and traditional Arab, and Bedouin culture. The influences on the region's architecture, music, fashion, cuisine and lifestyle are very prominent. Five times every day, Muslims are called to prayer from the

From top. Burj Al Arab ceiling. Sheikh Zayed Grand Mosque. Food market, Dubai. Souks. Sunset, Jumeirah Beach.

minarets of mosques which are scattered around the country. This is most fascinating to curious children. For families looking to stay in pure luxury, then the UAE offers outstanding accommodation options. The impressive number of super-luxury hotels are plentiful, most notably the sail-shaped Burj Al Arab (Tower of the Arabs), a Dubai landmark popularly known as a '7-star hotel' — a nonexistent category, but still opulent by any standard. The Emirates Palace in Abu Dhabi also aspires to the same standards, at a fraction of the price; both are impressive tourist destinations in their own right, and attract travellers in their droves.

The UAE is very accessible from Europe, and with regular flights from the UK, (only 6 hours) it is increasingly a firm favourite for families opting for a short and sunny winter break. Alternatively the UAE also makes as a great stop-over destination to visiting other parts of the world, such as Asia, Africa or Maldives.

🛏 **Fun Facts**

Capital: Abu Dhabi.

Population: 8.2 million.

Currency: UAE Dirham.

Languages: Arabic.

Trivia: Camel racing is the sport of Sheikhs (along with horse racing) and is the most popular spectator sport in the UAE.

Getting there and exploring around

Dubai and Abu Dhabi are the country's main international airports, though an increasing number of carriers are flying to Sharjah as well. There are also airports at Ras al-Khaimah, Fujairah and Al-Ain. Etihad (the National Airline) and Emirates (based in Dubai) both service the UAE, with regular flights from the UK and around the world. Both airlines have received many industry awards for their services, and offer strollers and high chairs at the airports and child packs to children in-flight, hence popular with travelling families.

There are good roads along the west coast between Abu Dhabi and Dubai, Sharjah and Ras al-Khaimah; between Sharjah and Dhaid. It is advisable though not to drive, as taxi's are plentiful (and can be hired with child seats) and the roads are quite hazardous.

Best time of year to visit

The UAE lies in the arid tropical zone extending across Asia and North Africa. Climatic conditions in the area are strongly influenced by the Indian Ocean, since the country borders both the Arabian Gulf and the Gulf of Oman. This explains why high temperatures in summer are always accompanied by high humidity along the coast. There are noticeable variations in climate between the coastal regions, the deserts of the interior and mountainous areas.

From November to March daytime temperatures average a very pleasant 24°C (75°F). Night-time temperatures are slightly cooler, averaging 13°C (56°F) and less than 5°C (40°F) in the depths of the desert or high in the mountains. Summer temperatures are very high, and can be as high as 48°C (118°F) inland, but it is lower by few degrees in coastal. Humidity in coastal areas averages between 50 and 60 per cent, touching over 90 per cent in summer and autumn. Inland it is far less humid. It's a good idea to avoid travelling to the UAE in the height of the summer (August), even though there are many air-conditioned shopping malls to keep children busy, outside activities will be limited as the extreme heat is very oppressive for young children.

The people of the UAE are vibrant and versatile and love to celebrate a number of festivals and events all round the year. From religious to cultural festivals to internationally renowned shopping and sports events, the annual calendar of the UAE is dotted with many festivals and events. The most popular festivals in the UAE include Ramadan, Eid Al Fitr and Eid Al Adha. Popular events in the country include the world-renowned Dubai Shopping Festival, National Day Festival, Dubai World Cup, Dubai Desert Classic, Dubai Summer Surprises, and Nokia Abu Dhabi International Jazz Festival.

FUN FAMILY FACT:

Falconry is among one of the many traditional pastimes which are still practiced. It is a unique partnership between man and bird and it is not unusual to see these hooded falcons being held and nurtured by their masters.

? Must know before you go

Drugs. The UAE takes a strict line on medicines, with many common drugs, notably anything with containing codeine, diazepam (Valium) or dextromethorphan (Robitussin) being banned unless you have a notarised and authenticated doctor's prescription. Visitors breaking the rules, even inadvertently, have found themselves deported or jailed. Be careful with children's medicines in particular.

Dress code. Etiquette is an important aspect of UAE culture and tradition, to which visitors are expected to conform. Recently, many expatriates have disregarded the law and been arrested for indecent clothing at beaches. Western-style dress is tolerated in appropriate places, such as bars or clubs, but the UAE has maintained a strict policy of protecting highly public spaces from cultural insensitivity.

Staying healthy. General medical care is quite good, with clinics for general and specialized care widely available, including some which are now open 24 hours. Call out private doctors in hotels offer a prompt service, even though this comes at a cost. The food is clean and in most restaurants is served to Western standards, particularly in tourist areas; however, hygiene can be an issue in some establishments outside, particularly roadside stalls. That said, food poisoning does happen, so use your common sense!

🎒 Highlights

Dubai Desert Thrill. Drive across the desert in a jeep taking in the spectacular scenery, landscapes and dine at 'Al Hadheerah' under the night sky.

Heritage in Abu Dhabi. Visit the 'Heritage Village' which showcases Abu Dhabi's rich cultural heritage and an interesting glimpse into the emirates past.

Rest in Ras al-Khaimah. Chill-out at your private poolside villa.

Swimming in Hatta. Explore the rock pools at the foot of the Hajar mountains.

👍 Tip for the Trip

"Research baby friendly cities in advance. Many developed destinations such as Dubai, have excellent facilities for babies, nappies, creams and toys can be found at the many shopping malls, so it's unnecessary to carry a lot of equipment with you."

Adventure:
Action + Adventure
Destination: Dubai

IDEAL FOR
ALL
AGES

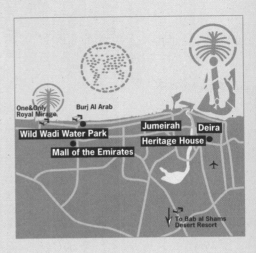

One&Only
Royal Mirage

Burj Al Arab

Wild Wadi Water Park

Jumeirah

Deira

Heritage House

Mall of the Emirates

To Bab al Shams
Desert Resort

✈ Regional Information

Dubai has all the ingredients for the perfect destination, culture, shopping and some serious action and adventure. With year round sunshine, beautiful beaches, stunning hotels and a rich Arabian culture, Dubai brings together all the elements needed for that family trip of a lifetime. It is also extremely well known for its warm hospitality and rich cultural heritage, and the Emirati people are welcoming and generous in their approach to visitors. It may not come cheap, but Dubai is an impressively indulgent destination.

Although Dubai is seen as a relatively young place, it has a fascinating history and a vibrant heritage that offers visitors an intriguing glimpse into Arabian culture. A good place to start exploring the history and heritage of Dubai is the Dubai Museum: it is located inside Al Fahidi Fort, one of Dubai's oldest buildings dating back to 1787. It was renovated in 1970 for use as a museum; further restoration and the addition of galleries were completed in 1995. Colourful and evocative dioramas, complete with life-size figures and sound and lighting effects, vividly depict everyday life in pre-oil days at the museum. Galleries show scenes from the creek, traditional Arab houses, mosques, the souk, date gardens, desert and marine life. One of the most interesting exhibits portrays the underwater world of pearl-diving, including sets of pearl merchants' weights, scales and sieves.

For enquiring minds, another fabulous historical spot is the delightful 'Heritage House', a free museum in Deira. It is a restored merchant's house from 1890, originally built by Mattar bin Saeed bin Muzaaina and is built in the traditional 'courtyard' style, and videos and mannequin set-ups display the original functions of each room (signs in English and Arabic). The staff seat you in the inner courtyard and serve a traditional mint tea (free) to get more of a taste of how it must have been to be rich and living in Dubai a hundred years ago. It is an outstanding exhibit in its own right, and close to the old 'souks' (markets) which can be visited at the same time.

United Arab Emirates '93

Adventure: Action + Adventure
Destination: Dubai

For action and adventure experiences, then it really doesn't get any better than Dubai. One of the most incredible day trips for a family is a 'desert safari.' There are many local companies who offer a variety of different versions of the desert experience from camel riding to taking a jeep or even sand-boarding for the ultimate adrenaline thrill. Sometimes a day trip can incorporate all 3 experiences. They usually end the day with an Arabic meal, shisha (although not one for children) and belly dancing. Overnight safari's offer an opportunity to not only experience a night under the stars, but also to observe the incredible nocturnal wildlife, such as gazelles and Arabian oryz.

For families with children of all ages, another incredible experience is taking a sea-plane around the gulf. There is a popular excursion called 'seawings' which is a 40 minute trip for up to nine passengers, providing views of Dubai's renowned landmarks including The Palm Jumeirah and The World Islands. It offers a fantastic and thrilling experience and a chance to appreciate the expanse of the city by sky.

No trip to Dubai with the family would be complete with a trip to the famous 'Wild Wadi' water park (Wadi is an Arabic term 'Valley'). This water theme park is 12 acres of pure, water based fun with 30 adrenalin-pumping rides and attractions including a surf wave and pools. It is extremely popular with locals too, (it gets busy in the hotter months) and is a fun experience for both young and old children.

If the sunshine gets too much, or in fact you are visiting in winter (which can get surprisingly cooler), then there are many indoor experiences to keep children happy. Ski Dubai is the first indoor ski resort in the Middle East and gives visitors the chance to enjoy skiing, snowboarding and tobogganing on real snow. From beginners to snow sport enthusiasts, Ski Dubai caters for all ages and ability levels. Then there is SEGA republic a five-zone entertainment adventure park with 9 roller coasters, and 150 amusement games spread over 2 levels – perfect for teenagers looking for that adrenalin rush! KidZania - a city made for children and run by children invites youngsters to take on 'real jobs' in a pint sized world. From flying a plane, to driving buses, working in restaurants, as a surgeon, dentist or shop assistant, kids 'run' the town, using their own currency. This mini city is 100% secure with children registered electronically when they enter the kingdom meaning parents can go and relax in a nearby cafe while their children play at being grown up.

Only a seven hour direct flight away, Dubai benefits from having only a three or four hour time difference with the UK/Ireland, meaning the jet lag many parents dread isn't a problem. Finally, it's safe, clean and you can find everything you may need, for even the smallest of babies, meaning and is perfect destination for all ages of children.

 Places to Stay

Bab Al Shams Desert Resort

An exclusive low-rise property in the desert surrounded by gently sloping dunes and natural desert landscape. Amazingly well equipped for children with a shaded pool, play room and activities such as riding on a camel are offered. The Al Hadheerah restaurant is a fabulous feast in the desert not to be missed.

Guide Price: From £187 prpn
Best Room: Royal suite with a ground floor patio

One&Only Royal Mirage

This place is heaven for families, it's a far cry from the 'hefty resorts' but it has all the trappings for children – a shaded pool, bikes, play areas. Its intimate courtyard setting, luxurious rooms and the crowing glory 'the oriental hammam' – a traditional Turkish bathing experience, is perfect for pampering parents too. Its idyllic location, a few steps from the famous sandy Jumeirah beach and the fabulous concierge-led service, attracts an affluent crowd, and locals love it too.

Guide Price: From £300 per suite per night
Best Room: The Palace double room

Burj Al Arab

The iconic 7-star sail doesn't need any introduction. Indulgent, luxurious and architecturally brilliant. Visitors arrive in their droves to gawp and photograph this masterpiece. Its oversized suites, with separate bathrooms, butler service and stunning views make it an inspiring place to stay. For young children and toddlers, the aquarium entrance, play room and small pool will be more than enough to keep them happy. A stay here, even if just a night or two, certainly provides the full, first class Arabian experience.

Guide Price: From £550 per suite per night
Best Room: All !

Places to Eat

Sezzam, Dubai

The three open kitchens at Sezzam create a vibrant atmosphere, and the restaurant also boasts entertainment areas including clowns and games which are great for children. Located overlooking the Ski Dubai slope and snow park, it's perfect for grabbing a delicious dish whether it's a fresh from the oven pizza or dim sum, there's something for everyone. Children under 6 years dine for free.

Baker & Spice, Dubai

This popular restaurant has a European heritage, with a Middle Eastern twist creating a unique and exciting menu which even the fussiest of children will enjoy. Set on a cooled terrace, the restaurant boasts views of the beautiful Dubai Fountain at the base of Burj Khalifa – the world's tallest tower.

Khan Murjan Restaurant, Dubai

At the heart of the souk (located in the WAFI city) is an exquisite marble courtyard, offering an oasis of cool serenity, yet open to the sky. The Umawi architecture provides an ornate backdrop to the social core of the souk, where families gather and dine. The restaurant here serves food made from only the freshest authentic ingredients, using traditional cooking techniques to create a menu that offers the delicious authentic Arabic taste.

Adventure: History + Culture
Destination: Abu Dhabi

IDEAL FOR
ALL
AGES

Dhow Harbour

Prego's

Al Hosn Palace

Marina Village

To Yas Island &
Ferrari Museum

Qusr el Bahr

Emirates Palace

To Qusr
al Sarab   Qaryat Al Beri

✈ Regional Information

Abu Dhabi, literally meaning the Father of Gazelle, is the second largest city of the United Arab Emirates in terms of population and frequently cited as being the richest city in the world. For families who want pure indulgence, fun museums and a spot of history and cultural experiences, then this is the city for them.

Heritage tours and sights are plentiful in Abu Dhabi. Starting with the Sheikh Zayed Grand Mosque, which is one of the largest mosques in the world. Complimentary 'walk-in' guided tours are available at 10am, 11am and 5pm daily (except Friday mornings). The tours, which are approximately 45-60 minutes, are led by Emirati guides who will take you and other visitors around the mosque interpreting various elements of the architecture, artistic elements and Islamic culture.

Abu Dhabi Heritage Village, which is situated near the Abu Dhabi Breakwater the village showcases Abu Dhabi's rich cultural heritage and an interesting glimpse into the emirates past. Traditional aspects of the desert way of life, including a campfire with coffee pots, a goats' hair tent are displayed in the open museum. There are also workshops where craftsmen demonstrate traditional skills, such as metal work and pottery, while women sit weaving and spinning.

Shopping is something of a national pastime in Abu Dhabi, perhaps because it's so diverse – everything from ultra-modern malls with the latest brands, to small, souk-like outlets where you can buy traditional perfumes, handicrafts, spices and carpets. You can spend thousands of dollars on a bejewelled designer watch, or pick up a basic timepiece in a supermarket. You can splash out on an haute-couture designer outfit or buy fabric and have a local tailor make up your very own creation for a bargain price. Prices are often excellent in comparison to those abroad, especially for carpets, textiles and gold. If you are good at bargaining, you can get even better deals. Children will enjoy the diversity of stalls and haggling in the souks, just make sure you keep a close eye on very young children from wandering off on their own.

Adventure: History + Culture
Destination: Abu Dhabi

When fully opened, The Souk at Central Market will offer more than 250 shops in one setting.

Ferrari World, located on Yas Island, opened in 2012 will get children's and heads and hearts racing. The world's largest indoor theme park. Created around the classic double-curve body shell design of a Ferrari car, the park features over 20 thrilling rides and attractions, including the world's fastest rollercoaster, Formula Rossa, which powers to 240 km/h in less than five seconds. There is an exciting Junior Grand Prix area - a racing school for budding Scuderia drivers who can drive child-sized Ferrari F1 racers, plus many Italian dining options in the park to fill hungry tummies.

Further afield is Al Ain (meaning 'the spring) which makes a great destination for a day trip for the family. There is a superb Wildlife Park covering 900 hectares near the foot of Jebel Hafeet. This vast resort features towers of giraffes, herds of zebras and crashes of rhinoceroses, all co-existing in the mixed African-inspired exhibit. Enjoy watching the fabulous rare white lions of Sambona. Elsewhere, indigenous Arabian Oryx and gazelle offer a glimpse of wildlife typical to the local region and abundance of green public spaces are ideal picnic spots; there are also children's playgrounds and a special train tour of the wildlife area.

The Al Ain Palace Museum (also known as the Qasr Al Ain Museum), which was once the home of late Sheikh Zayed Bin Sultan Al Nahyan and was also a hub of the city's political life. Here you will enjoy a unique experience discovering a large collection of material concerning the ruling family such as portraits of the royal family, a family tree depicting the Sheikh's lineage, and a schoolroom, where the royal children received their education from private tutors.

The camel market is one of the areas you shouldn't miss. Here, children get the chance to explore those enormous animals which are kept in a series of fenced paddocks according to their intended use. Young camels, reared for meat, are separated from older animals kept for breeding and milk. Most people enjoy hearing lively, the traders mentioning the merits of their prized animals, discussing prices and negotiating sales.

Finally for slightly older children a hot air balloon expedition into the desert is a must. Enjoy a ride over the giant red sand dunes, emerald green oases, gazelles and camels. The balloon adventure, takes off at approximately 4.30am from a desert oasis north of Al Ain, transportation from Abu Dhabi is provided free of charge. Balloon expeditions are from September – May.

There is such an incredible variety of experiences for families staying in Abu Dhabi, and which can be used as a base to explore other parts of the UAE.

Place to Stay

Qaryat Al Beri
A 'Shangri-La' run property featuring all the luxuries expected with this well-known chain. All 214 rooms and suites are generous in size and are decorated with an Arabian flavour. Rooms on the upper floors are more private and some offer views of the shimmering new Sheikh Zayed Mosque.

Guide Price: From £95 prpn
Best Room: Speciality Suite with separate lounge and entertainment area

Qusr Al Sarab Desert Resort
The Anantara Resort & Spa Qasr Al Sarab is an oasis an hour and a half outside of Abu Dhabi, in the middle of the Liwa Desert. Perfectly orientated to take in classic desert valley, mountainous sands and the sunset, its luxurious and refined – yet a haven with children.

Guide Price: From £252 prpn
Best Room: Two-bedroom villa with a plunge pool

Emirates Palace
This isn't a small boutique hotel – quite the opposite – a huge sprawl of 1,000,000m² with east and west wings catering for the mass tourist market. But for families (especially young ones) this hotel is a palace dream. From the outside it feels like you are entering a Sheikh's private palace residence, from the inside it's opulent and the suites are over generous.

Guide Price: From £357 prpn
Best Room: The Khaleej & Khaleej Deluxe suite

Places to Eat

Marrakesh, Abu Dhabi
Savour authentic Moroccan cuisine at this opulent restaurant, while enjoying a belly dancer and Moroccan band playing. The lemon chicken tagine is a favourite.

Prego's, Abu Dhabi
Located at 'Rotana Beach Hotel' is always atmospheric and busy. The seafood linguine is amazing. Sit on the terrace and enjoy delicious olive tapenade, hot breads and wood fired pizzas.

Awtar, Abu Dhabi
One of the more authentic eateries in the capital, serving fresh 'mezes' and baked saj loafs. A late dinner here is a spectacle with a nightly performance by exuberant belly dancer. Friendly Lebanese waiters add to the vibrant atmosphere.

Adventure: Reflect + Re-new
Destination: Ras al-Khaimah

JUNIOR 7-11 TEEN 12-16

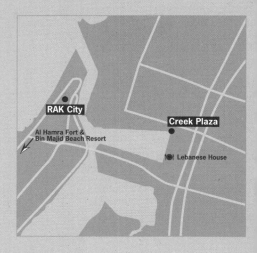

RAK City

Creek Plaza

Al Hamra Fort & Bin Majid Beach Resort

Lebanese House

Regional Information

Ras al-Khaimah is the northern most emirate of the UAE, often referred to as 'the wild west', a favourite weekend getaway for people from Dubai, and it is an up-coming tourist destination. It has two cities, Ras al-Kaimah old town on a sandy peninsula along the gulf coast and Al-Nakheel, the newer business district. It is a fairly charming place and makes an excellent, chilled-out family destination with older children.

Ras al-Khaimah has an impressive archaeological heritage and a very rich history. This area had always enticed settlers with its unique combination of all the four types of landscapes found in different parts of the United Arab Emirates: the fertile plains, the mountainous region, coastal areas and the desert environment.

Things to do in RAK, (as it is often referred to) are fairly low-key, with the emphasis being on rest and relaxation. However, the Ras al-Khaimah's museum is in the old fort on Al-Hosen road, (next to police station), which makes an interesting visit. The Museum was constructed in 1987 and is located at Al Husen Fort which was the residence of the Sheikh during the 19th century. Old Manuscripts including treaties signed by the ruling family with the British are on display in the museum. Antiques and Islamic objects d'art are displayed as well. Some of these date back to 5th millennium B.C. The Museum has different winter and summer times as well as a different schedule during Ramadan which is the Muslim holy month of fasting.

The old town is a lovely place to wander, especially the Souq area (market) south of the museum which has an authentic, un-touristy feel to it. RAK pearls can be purchased here, which are known globally for their quality. The pearl farm is the UAE's only organised cultured pearl farm and is trying to help the country reclaim its role in the pearl industry. It was well known that the peoples of the Gulf States in the past depended on diving for natural pearls for a living until the Japanese discovered the technology for growing cultured pearls in the early twentieth century. As a consequence, the natural pearl trade receded in the Gulf, causing the demise of the diving and pearling industry.

Adventure: Reflect + Re-new
Destination: Ras al-Khaimah

The pearl farm is trying to culture pearls again, so by buying a RAK pearl you would be helping to re-build this industry.

Around Ras al-Khaimah there are plenty of attractions. For culture vultures Shimal (which is approximately 5 kilometres north) is a site of some of the most important archaeological finds in the UAE. The site comprises a number of proto-historic settlement remains, a very extensive contemporaneous cemetery and a medieval fortress locally known as the 'Palace of the Queen of Sheba'. The area has been settled for at least 4500 years and its former inhabitants have benefited from its favourable setting close to the sea, pastures and cultivable lands. A half day drive to Shimal is definitely worth a trip.

There are plenty of experiences in RAK and its surrounds if you want a relaxing family break, but equally if your children get itchy feet there are several 'outdoors experiences'.

Like its neighbouring Emirates, RAK offers a trip to the sand dunes in a four wheel drive. A drive in the dunes can be extremely exciting and can be combined with a visit to a Camel Farm. The desert safari gives one a chance to observe the lives of the Bedouin people. The Bedouins are a nomadic tribe who live in the desert. These Bedouins work at the various Camel Farms where racing camels are bred for a sporting tradition that has been handed down from generations. RAK has also has an excellent 10 kilometre camel racing track.

Then there are wonderful Dhow cruises in Musandam. These cruises traverse coastal villages and afford opportunities for swimming and snorkelling amongst the languid dolphin inhabited waters. Again a lovely experience for families.

Finally, at the Khatt Springs, there are therapeutic spring waters which attract many tourists. They are in the mountains of RAK and are composed of three natural springs which have hot (almost 40°C) waters which are thought to have medicinal value. Palm trees encircle the area and enhance the natural beauty of the springs. The area is also famous for a large number of archeological sites which bear witness to the old civilizations which inhabited the region.

🛏️ 🍴 Place to Stay and Eat

Banyan Tree Al Wadi

Opened in January 2010, Banyan Tree Al Wadi is the first desert resort in the UAE to offer a concept of all-pool villas, in a dedicated nature reserve and a private beach setting. They have a stunning spa for stressed out parents (and older teenagers) offering the very best Asian treatments, including a hammam and numerous water based therapies. There is also an incredible 18-hole championship golf course. In terms of activities for all children, they offer horse riding, camel riding, falconry centre and bike trails. There is also a nice kids club for aged 4 years and upwards who offer educational activities such as stories under the stars and camel milking. It is situated on 100 hectares of enchanting desert playground and approximately 45 minutes from Dubai airport - though the beach villas are 20 minute drive from the main resort.

Best Room: Al Rimal Deluxe Pool Villa with a living area and sofa bed
Guide Price: From £400 per villa per night

Lebanese House

Located next to the Hilton Hotel, is this Lebanese restaurant. Everything is excellent at this restaurant. They offer a great range of hummous, lentil soup, kebabs, and mixed grill, so there is something for every palate. They even do a take-away service!

Opposite page. Hatta Fort with Hajar Mountain backdrop.

Focus On...
Hatta

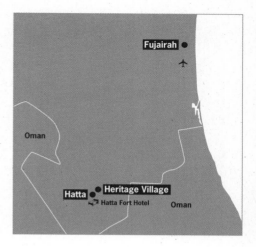

45 million year ago Hatta was covered with water, now Hatta nestles in the shadows of the Hajar mountain range, 100 kilometre from the coast. It is an ancient oasis village high in the mountains to the east of Dubai, which makes an excellent place to stay for a couple of days. The fortified city of Hatta huddles around an ancient ruined citadel, like some medieval flock with the beautiful Wadi Hatta, an area of ponds and lakes, fig groves and mosque towers.

Historically, Hatta was at one time a vital Omani border post. It was an important camel trail along Sohar, Dibba and Muscat, and commanded one of the three gateways through Oman's mountain chain – a true Bedouin civilization. Just 20 years ago the people of Hatta used camels as the only means of transport and a trip to Dubai meant a five-day journey.

Hatta village is over 200 years old and dotted with houses of stone, sand and mud, both big and small, which silently speak of the life. Unfortunately, most of the houses in the old part of the village have fallen into ruins as the materials used did not stand up to the test of time.

Another of the town's landmarks is the recently built fort standing at a crossing just at the entrance of the town and the Hatta Fort Hotel. It is a remarkable piece of architecture and it captures in many details the medieval ramparts. Complete with 80 acres of well-manicured gardens, fine dining, and various leisure activities including a wonderful spa and wellness centre, this mountain retreat is for rest and rejuvenation.

While in Hatta there are a variety of things to do. The Hatta Heritage Village which you can explore Bedouin life and culture and the Hatta Pools which are a group of fissures that run through the valley amid the Hajar Mountains. The Pools are a dramatic sight, hidden from view until you reach them. Hatta is the UAE's most popular spot for wadi driving, and it's common to see convoys of families and youths hooning about in 4x4s. The rocky crevices, natural water pools and palm oases make for an atmospheric drive, and the proximity to Dubai (around one hour) makes it a good choice for a day trip or an overnight stay. Out of towners can drive for a couple of hours, stop off for a picnic and a plunge at Hatta Pools, nose about the Heritage Village and spend the night at Hatta Fort Hotel or pitch a tent under the stars..

ⓘ Stylish Essentials

Ras al-Khaimah

Official Tourism Division
www.raktourism.com

Ras al-Khaimah Museum
www.rakmuseum.gov.ae

Pearl Farm
www.rakpearls.com/pearlfarms.html

Banyan Tree
PO Box 35288 Al Mazraa,
Ras al-Khaimah,
UAE
www.banyantree.com
T. +971 (0) 7206 7777
E. reservations-alwadi@banyantree.com

Lebanese House
Muntasir Road
Beside Nakheel Hotel,
Ras al-Khaimah,
UAE
T. +971 (0) 7228 9992

Hatta

Hatta Fort Hotel
PO Box 9277
Dubai
United Arab Emirates
www.hattaforthotel.com
T. +971 (0) 4 809 9333

Turkish Gulet.

TURKEY

Ionian Coast | Lycian Coast | Istanbul | Cappadocia

TURKEY

Romania Ukraine Russia
Bulgaria Black Sea Georgia
Istanbul
★ Ankara
● Cappadocia
● Bodrum
● Antalya
Cyprus Iraq
Mediterranean Syria
Sea Lebanon

🏆 Why is this place so special?

Turkey is fast becoming one of the most popular family holiday destinations in the world; although in certain tourist areas it has a reputation for a 'package holiday hotspot', it has an abundance of authentic, exciting adventures for the independent traveller. Turkish people genuinely love children and they will receive affection everywhere, treating them like royalty and therefore making the whole family feel very welcome to this country.

Turkey is the most southern and most sunny of all European countries and the almost endless Mediterranean coastline has some of the best beaches and coastline scenery in the world. It is also a country which links East with West. It is where Europe meets Asia and this exciting mix is seen in everything from culture to cooking. All the main Western Empires have risen and fallen here - the Romans, Greeks, Persians and Byzantines, leaving behind splendid ruins which are better preserved here than almost anywhere else.

One of the joys of Turkey is the food. It is true fusion of Greek, Persian and Middle Eastern foods, and one of the best ways of sampling this is to head to a local restaurant for a 'Meze'. The portions, which be shared with the family are all child size and there are sure to be least a few dishes children will like. Sharing food and eating is such a family orientated past-time and its not unusual to see families (even with very young children) eating in restaurants late at night.

The coastline stretches over 1600 kilometres, and is divided up into four divisions - the Ionian Coast for its history, the Carian Coast for its beauty, the West Lycian Coast for its wild rugged terrain and the East Lycian Coast for its mountainous crags and ancient tombs. The weather and sailing conditions are calm along almost the entire coast, making it even more perfect for a sailing adventure for the family.

A visit to at least one major town in Turkey is a must to capture the flavour of the Middle East. And Istanbul is the top of that list. Its narrow streets and alleyways are

buzzing with life with outdoor cafes, shops and restaurants all contributing to the sights and spicy smells. All roads lead to the Grand Bazaar that is packed with as many as 30,000 traders offering an exotic array of kaftans, carpets and copper ware. Children will marvel and enjoy haggling here.

Although there are a score of archeological sites in Turkey worth seeing, a visit to Cappadocia is a real treat. Families can spend a day enjoying the views over-ground in a hot air balloon or explore the many underground cities, such as the Derinkuyu underground city. It's a bit of a trek for just a day, so spending a night in one of the 'cave' hotels can really add to the experience.

Whether you are walking the cities, sailing the coastline or ballooning over the mountains, Turkey is a seriously special destination for a family adventure. Although it may not be easy travelling with very young children or toddlers, it really offers much excitement, education and fun for older children and teenagers.

Fun Facts

Capital: Ankara.

Population: 72 million.

Currency: Turkish Lira.

Languages: Turkish.

Trivia: Istanbul is the only city in the world located on two continents, Europe and Asia. In its thousands of years of history, it has been the capital of three great empires - Roman, Byzantine and Ottoman.

✈ Getting there and exploring around

Turkey is approximately 4 hours journey by air from the UK making it a great choice for a city break or a longer family trip. Unless you are travelling as part of a package holiday most flights will be to or via Istanbul, the country's largest city and the gateway to the country. There are some direct flights from the UK to other Turkish cities, particularly during the summer months when both scheduled and charter flights operate direct services.

Turkish Airlines (the national airline), British Airways, Pegasus Airlines, EasyJet and Jet2, all operate scheduled services from the UK to Istanbul, landing at either Ataturk International Airport on the European side of the city or at the new and smaller Sabiha Gökcen Airport on the Asian shore. Most flights depart from London airports; however, Turkish Airlines also have direct flights from Birmingham, Manchester and Dublin.

Taksim is the transport hub of Istanbul and from there you can jump in a taxi or take the metro or a bus to your final destination. The signature yellow taxis are also always on stand-by as an alternative, though a more costly alternative journey into town. Taxis all have taxi meters with a standard rate across the whole country, with a night rate applicable between midnight and 6am. Flights are available from the UK direct to many other cities in Turkey, with regular flights to Antalya, Bodrum, and Dalaman, airports close to popular holiday resorts, but in most other instances you will need to transfer via Istanbul.

Getting around Turkey is easy, although there are regular domestic flights connecting all major cities; Turkey also has a great bus and train network. Travelling by train means you'll have a bed, your own room, a restaurant for meal times and is a much more comfortable way to travel. The main train operator in Turkey is TCDD, which was originally built by the Germans, has recently been majorly improved and trains can now travel at speeds up to 95mph. There are no trains directly to Antalya, Marmaris, Bodrum, Alanya, nor to Goreme so use a combination of train and bus to reach these destinations. Train travel in Turkey can be a wonderful experience, and bunking down on 4-berth couchettes can be a lot of fun for children too.

☼ Best time of year to visit

The climate in Turkey is influenced by its eastern location and by the sea that surrounds it. Summers are very hot and humid in some areas, (reaching a sweltering 45°C in August) and can be particularly hot in the major cities. At altitude, however, the nights can be quite cool, especially in the winter months. On the Black Sea Coast, the climate is almost tropical in some respects and the vegetation is very dense.

Istanbul itself is really a year round destination (although perhaps in the very height of the summer sun it may be uncomfortable for children). The many historical sights, museums and bazaars can be explored at any time of the year. For the rest of the country, and the coastline, if summer sunshine is what you are looking for then discover the country during the months of May and June, or September and October for the best conditions, both in terms of climate and prices.

? Must know before you go

Shopping tips. Shop owners often offer home-made tea when you enter their shop, but you should decline if you don't plan to buy anything. Stores are generally open between 7am and 7pm, sometimes with a break mid-afternoon.

Food on the hop. Turkey is a foodie heaven, offering everything from sticky sweet 'baklava' to smoky kebabs. Although most restaurants welcome children, few will have highchairs or baby changing facilities. If you are out and about, there are many fast food healthy options such as 'sweet corn stands' and 'fresh fruit smoothies', which can fill tummies without the need to stop in the day.

Learn the lingo. Making an effort with the Turkish language can go a long way to building a relationship with locals and its fun learning for children too. It isn't a simple language to learn but phrases such as 'Merhaba' (Hello), Günaydın (Good morning) and Tesekkür ederim (Thank-you) will be appreciated.

Highlights

Ionian Coast. Discover beautiful harbours, fresh seafood and stunning archaeological sites.

Sail the Lycian Coast. Hire a crew and a Turkish gulet and set sail for the seas of the Lycian Coastline.

Souks of Istanbul. Souvenir shopping at Istanbul's Grand Bazaar and Spice Bazaar and marvel at the some of the best street traders in the world.

Cappadocia Caves. Hot air balloon riding over the chimneys of Cappadocia and spend the night in a cave.

FUN FAMILY FACT:

Contrary to popular opinion, tulip originated not in Holland but in Turkey. The Turks first gave the Dutch their famous tulips that started the craze for the flower in England and the Netherlands. There is a period of elegance and amusement in 17th century is named The Tulip Age in Ottoman Empire.

Tip for the Trip

"Always check visa requirements in advance of travelling, as this will save you the headache of queuing on arrivals – and with tired, bored children this can be a recipe for disaster. The visa system for Turkey can be both relatively simple and mind-bogglingly complicated at the same time. There is no 'one size fits all' approach, with the availability of visas, type of visas, and the cost all different depending on your nationality. Contact the Turkish consulate in your country before you travel to obtain one in advance"

Adventure: Food + Discovery
Destination: Ionian Coast

IDEAL FOR
ALL
AGES

Port Saip •   • Foça

Mezza Luna
• Izmir

• Çesme   • Urla

• Sigacik

Greek Waters

Samos

Asin •

Kempinski
Hotel Barbaros
& Amanruya

Bodrum

✛ Regional Information

The Ionian coast extends from Izmir in the north - where it meets the Aeolian coast - until Bodrum in the south where it borders with the Carian coast. The coastline boasts one of the best climates in the whole of Turkey, and flourishing culture and history to match. Highlights of this region lie within the harbours and anchorages of Izmir, Foça, Urla, Port Saip, Çesme, Sigacik, Kusadasi, Asin, Gulluk, Torba and Bodrum as well as the stunning archaeological sites of Teos, Ephesus, Latmos, Didyma and Gümüslük. Families with children of all ages can enjoy this region, and you can easily spend a week or two exploring and discovering the coastline in several ways.

Turkey is surrounded by turquoise waters of the four seas, the Mediterranean, the Aegean, the Black Sea and the Sea of Marmara. Its indented coastline provides splendid bays, coves, inlets and different anchorages where families can enjoy various water sport activities; swimming, diving, waterskiing, fishing, or simply experience the cultural heritage of the ancient cities and surroundings. The Ionian coast is particularly ideal for yacht charter holidays like (bareboat) charters and gulet charters, due to secluded coves and calm waters or for the more adventurous you can easily approach the Eastern Sporades (Greece) as well as the Dodecanese Islands starting from one of the bases on the Ionian coast to extend your trip. Sailing trips can be organised locally or through travel companies before travelling, and charters can be hired privately with a crew.

However, the best way to truly experience the coast is by combining sailing and sightseeing. The coast is home to some spectacular sights, remains of ancient civilizations, medieval castles, stone fortresses, and even marble palaces.

Izmir, is the third most populous city in Turkey and has the country's largest port (after Istanbul). It makes a great starting point for travelling around this area, and spending a night or two to explore the regions highlights before boarding a Turkish gulet. On of the most interesting places to visit in Izmir is to take a ride up to the

Adventure: Food + Discovery
Destination: Ionian Coast

mountain park in the Teleferik (Cable Car). At the top there is a large lake view where you can have BBQ in the pine forests. Shops, bars and restaurants are available. So if you decide to have a BBQ you can buy your meat, vegetables and bread from the shops at the top, and have the charcoal BBQ set up for you by the park staff.

Foça is a charming town close to Izmir, and set around two anchoring bays, known as 'Big Sea' and 'Little Sea' and is renowned for its excellent seafood restaurants particularly calamari and sea bass which are served among the many seafront restaurants. The 'Siren song' legend has it that the Siren Cliffs on Orak Island, off the coast of Foça, were once home to the Sirens. With their beautiful songs, the Sirens would lure sailors to their deaths on the cliffs. In ancient art, the Sirens are often depicted as mermaids, so it's possible that the sirens were none other than Foca's playful monk seals. These days, travellers can take a daily boat trip from Kucukdeniz to Orak Island, and stop for swimming breaks along the way. Other sights worth visiting are the Seytan Hamami (Satan's Bath) – a tomb like structure at the foot of the Can Peak, 2 kilometres from Foça, and the Bes Kapilar Castle (the Castle of 5 gates) which is used as an open-air theatre.

Çesme, meaning 'fountain' in Turkish, is a much smaller port and home to Turkey's most beautiful stretches of beach. In the natural bays you can swim in absolute peace. Many lovely bays, accessible only by yacht, stretch along the coast southeast of the town and ensure peaceful and relaxing anchorages in this popular sailing region. The sea at Alacati also has ideal conditions for windsurfing since it is exposed to high winds. There is also a windsurfing school on the quay here that holds courses for beginners. Cark Beach is a favourite with families with young children because the sea is shallow.

Along the coast there lies Sigacik, which is close to the archeological site of Teos. Sigacik is a magnet for windsurfers, sailors and, less predictably, rock climbers attracted by the challenge of towering cliffs on a small island. Teos was founded in 1050-1000 B.C., one of twelve Ionian cities. The people of Teos built magnificent architectural monuments, such as the Temple of Dionysus which stands at the edge of the road. The temple was built at the beginning of the 2nd century B.C. by Hermogenes of Priene and is the largest of all temples to Dionysus in Turkey. It was repaired several times during Roman times but fresh earthquakes took their toll. A walking along the paved road of Teos and a visit to the temples is definitely worth a stop here.

Bodrum is a very popular resort and yachting port, it may be well-known as a tourist hotspot, (and its nightlife) but loud music set aside, it boasts the ruins of the original Mausoleum, one of the seven wonders of the world, as well as the lofty castle of St. Peter a crusader fortress which now serves as the worlds foremost Museum of Underwater Archaeology, and a Greco Roman theatre (which is spectacular during sunset). As Bodrum is a major yachting port, if you are not staying aboard a sailing vessel, families can easily rent a yacht by the day and cruise the Bodrum peninsular, stopping off for a lunch or a swim.

Places to Stay

4Reasons, Yalikavak

Funky, minimalist and modern sums up this family friendly property near Bodrum. '4 reasons' stands for – serenity, design, quality, attitude, which the hotels excels on all accounts. By day, you can hop on a gulet cruise, get a day pass to one of the beach clubs, go horse-riding or watersporting, or explore Bodrum castle. Children of all ages are actively welcomed and you can book baby-sitters and cots.

Guide Price: From £120 per suite per night
Best Room: Junior Suites have a sitting area with a sofa (doubles as extra bed for one child)

Kempinski Hotel Barbaros Bay, Bodrum

A commanding view over the Aegean Sea, combined with a magnificent architecture. It has 148 rooms and 25 suites, and unspoiled natural beauty surrounding the bay, the hotel has pretty much everything for a family who want to be looked after. Families can take a cruise on a Turkish Gulet or learn to Scuba Dive, and there is an on-site kids & teen studio.

Guide Price: From £130 prpn
Best Room: One bedroom suite with 2 bathrooms

Amanruya, Bodrum

Due to open fully in early 2012, the latest addition to the super luxury 'Aman' chain. This is no ordinary resort by any means; anyone who visits an 'Aman' property is hooked for life. Amanruya is surrounded by a pine forest and olive groves, and is set on a peaceful hillside in Mandalya Bay with views of the sea and a winding path to a protected pebble beach. They offer excursions to the ancient ruins and mountain biking or horse riding.

Guide Price: From £650 for a pool terrace cottage per night
Best Room: The only room is the pool terrace cottage, spacious enough for 2 adults and 2 children

Places to Eat

Mezza Luna, Izmir

Popular with locals, this Italian eatery is cosy and friendly. Situated at the end of Konak Pier, with great views of the sea. Snacks and salads are served all day but the chef's talents shine in the evening, the decor is nautical outside with up-market Italian furnishings inside.

Otantik Ocakbasi, Bodrum

A friendly Turkish restaurant, set a street away from the main tourist street and the seafront, yet feels a world apart. The Turkish 'meze' dishes are huge, and sharing a plate is more than ample for a family. They will also deliver by scooter to anywhere in Bodrum however some Turkish is required to organise the delivery over the phone.

Maça Kizi Restaurant, Bodrum

In service since 2000 in Gültürkbükü, Maça Kızı Restaurant is preferred for mantı (ravioli-like dish served with yogurt) and baklava, which are cooked fresh in the stone oven. An open buffet is available for lunch, much to the delight of children, and dinner is served under olive trees outside.

Adventure:
Education + Hands On
Destination: Lycian Coast

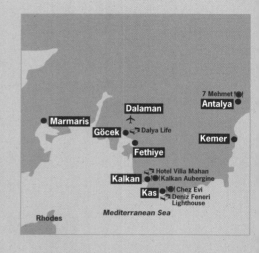

✛ Regional Information

The Lycian coast is named after the many Lycian cities dotted along its shores. The stretch from Marmaris to Göcek forms the western part of the whole Lycian coast and it extends further east towards Antalya, covering Fethiye, Kas, and Kalkan.

The west Lycian Coast from Marmaris to Fethiye, is known as 'the pirate coast' with its wild, mountainous shores and hundreds of hidden coves, ripe for exploration. The east Lycian Coast from Fethiye, running through Kas, Kalkan and Antalya, are abound with rock tombs, and mountainous ranges.

Sailing along the coastline has become such an incredible past time for many travellers here and increasingly for families. Travellers usually start their cruises at Izmir, Bodrum, Marmaris, Fethiye or Antalya - these not only being the largest ports along the coastline and the locations where many chartered cruises leave from, but are also (for the most part) the cities that mark the limits of each section of the coastline. From one of these locations, it is as simple as choosing a direction and moving along the coast - and of course having the requisite charts, or a local guide, so as to ensure you do not get lost or damage your boat.

Many people like to start and end their cruises in Marmaris, simply because it is the largest sailing and yacht charter hub on the entire coastline - not only this, it is also a resort area, with for most of the part, nice beaches. Because of its popularity, you can get a really good deal on a luxurious apartment or hotel and have a cheap holiday in Marmaris before (or after) your cruise begins. Learning to sail can add really to the experience of a lifetime for children over the age of 12, who can participate in the RYA practical courses, such as 'competent crew' for the complete beginner. The courses usually last 5 days to 1 week and families can sleep on-board during their time, with opportunities to swim and snorkel too. There are several companies along the Lycian who offer these courses, but particularly in Göcek.

Opposite page. **Left.** Nature spa, Fethiye.
Right. Kalkan Aubergine, courtesy of
Kalkan Aubergine.

Adventure: Education + Hands On
Destination: Lycian Coast

Göcek which recently became the meeting point of yachtsmen and lovers of the sea, has attained a justified fame with its natural position. Since 1988, the region has been declared a special environmental protection area and as a result has become a third degree natural site. In the waters near the Forest Department administration section in the vicinity of Göcek a breakwater and a variety of old remains can be observed. The old name of Göcek is Kalinche and in nearby coves, like in this one, many other old remains can be seen. These remains are a proof of these coves having been used in earlier times. Göcek remains fairly unspoiled: there are only a handful of small hotels, yet all along the wide, landscaped promenade that fringes the quayside, there are plenty of eateries, from simple cafes to excellent restaurants specialising in delicious fresh fish. In the back streets and around the old village square by the mosque, there is a surprising array of interesting craft shops.

Further along the coast there is the very touristy resort of Fethiye, like many of the Turkish ports, was once a quiet fishing village, which can become a touristic town overnight. Although there maybe little in terms of authentic accommodation, if you are on a yacht you can take full advantage of the stunning coves and coastline with beautiful hilltop forests which are simply incredible.

Kalkan is famous for its white-washed houses to the sea, and is considered fairly upmarket and charming. The historic harbour is situated at the foot of the Taurus Mountain, and the town overlooks a beautiful bay. Unlike a few other Turkish coastal resort towns Kalkan's main economy is tourism – but its citizens put much pride and effort into the town's historic preservation. Because of this, Kalkan has retained the texture of its history by protecting its distinctive Ottoman Greek architecture (it was once an Ottoman Greek and Turkish fishing village). Very strict building codes keep the town small and architecturally blended with the historic heart of the town known as 'Old Kalkan'.

On the road stretching from Kalkan through Kas to Antalya is the stunning backdrop of the 'Taurus Mountains', which is divided up into 4 ranges and has peaks stretching above 12,000 ft. There are many ways to experience the mountains, from a 2 hour quad biking experience to cycling and walking. There are also two ski resorts on the mountain range, one at Davras about 25 kilometres (16 miles) from the two nearest towns of Egirdir and Isparta, the second is Saklıkent 40 kilometres (25 miles) from the city of Antalya.

Finally the Lycian journey ends in Antalya, which is one of the most beautiful provinces on the coast. It is an attractive, modern city with shady palm-lined boulevards, a prize-winning marina, and a picturesque 'old quarter', with narrow winding streets and old wooden houses in the ancient city walls. There are many historic sites in the region, which makes Antalya a good base to stay, such as Aspendos (only 50 kilometre east of Antalya), which was an important centre of trade during Roman times. Today, the most impressive aspect of Aspendos is the stunning theatre, which was built in approx. 162 A.D. It seats 15,000 and has been beautifully preserved. Each year it hosts the Aspendos Opera and Ballet Festival which takes place in June and July and gives you the opportunity to see performances of classics in a magnificent setting.

Dalya Life, Göcek

Dalya Life is a small, simple 'organic' hotel in a gorgeous valley, situated along a stream and surrounded by groves of liquid amber trees - nature lovers will enjoy this tranquil hideaway. Only 10-minutes from Göcek. This family-run chic retreat has a warm & friendly atmosphere, with delicious traditional food. Extra beds / baby cots for children aged 0-12 are free of charge.

Guide Price: From £80 prpn
Best Room: Newly refurbished garden suite with living room and verandah

Hotel Villa Mahal, Kalkan

Super stylish boutique hotel, located across the bay from the main harbour at Kalkan. The sea front position has outstanding panoramic views, and with just 13 rooms which spread across the hillside, gives the place a quiet, atmosphere. Steps lead to a terrace overlooking the sea, where breakfast is taken. Choose from an array of local yoghurt, honey, fruits, pancakes and home-made jams. They offer a free boat shuttle service to Kalkan harbour. Suitable for children over 9 years old.

Guide Price: From £200 prpn
Best Room: Cliff House, a one bedroom villa with pool laid out over two-stories

Deniz Feneri Lighthouse, Kas

The 28-bedroom water front hotel has sweeping coastal views and some awe-inspiring sunsets. There is a small children's pool with the benefit of a sun shade, and children will have fun in the reading and games area. Here you'll find various board games, satellite television, DVDs and a Playstation.

Guide Price: From £800 per week
Best Room: Waterfront suite, 1 bedroom villa sleeping 1-4 guests

Kalkan Aubergine, Kalkan

The Aubergine restaurant has been in business since 1995. Over the years, it has become one of the most popular places to eat in Kalkan. Located by the harbour, it now has 70 covers, plus a number of chill-out sofas for those wanting just a drink. As the aubergine (patlıcan), is a popular vegetable in Turkey, and is featured in many traditional dishes, so they named the restaurant after it.

7 Mehmet, Antalya

This is another phenomenal restaurant in Antalya, situated in Ataturk Kultur Parki. It serves great Turkish and Antalian cuisine, and offers great view of the city. The restaurant menu includes meat entrees, tandoor kebab, fresh salads, mezes and great selection of wines. Don't miss out on the tripe soup, which may sound a bit too exotic, but really tastes great.

Chez Evi, Kas

This is the best meal you will have in Turkey, not only for the food, but also for the eccentricity of the chef. A typically French restaurant which offers crepes and salads, and one mean chicken curry. Popular dishes are the calmars à la Provençale (calamari in a spicy tomato sauce) and the filet de boeuf sauce champignons (steak in a mushroom sauce).

Adventure: History + Culture
Destination: Istanbul

To Hotel Les Ottomans & Çiragan Palace Kempinski

● Taksim Square

Beyoglu   *Bosphorus*

|●! Tere Kebab

Neorian Hotel   ● Topaki Palace
Grand Bazaar ●
● Sultanahmet
● Blue Mosque

To Atatürk Airport

Regional Information

Istanbul, a fascinating and beautiful city built on two continents and divided by the Bosphorus Strait. It is one of the greatest destinations on the planet where you can see a modern western city combined with traditions of the east. Inhabited for at least 5,000 years, it was capital to two of the world's most powerful empires – the Byzantines and the Ottomans – which have certainly left their imprints on the ancient city.

Discovering the highlights are easy (yet sometimes overwhelming) but you can cover the major attractions within a couple of days, which make it a perfect destination for long weekenders or as an introductory stopover to elsewhere in Turkey. Visiting Istanbul with children is a wonderful experience, and older ones will be wowed by the opulent Topkapi Palace, great churches and mosques, ancient city walls, and colourful bazaars.

Anyone visiting the city must stop by the 'Topkapi Palace' (located at Seraglio point) a palace which was built for a sultan and several of his wives. Not only was this a palace for royalty but it was also the Ottoman's Empire centre of government for 400 years. The decorative rooms, museum and courtyards are extensive so you should definitely allow a full day for the visit. The imperial wardrobe inside the palace maybe particularly interesting for children, a collection of over 3,000 elaborately embroidered royal robes, and the treasury of jewel-encrusted swords and daggers, which is equally magnificent.

The 'Blue Mosque' is one of the world's most famous religious buildings and is simply a work of art. The main dome and columns (which are beautifully lit at night) can be seen for many miles away. The mosque is located in Sultanahmet, which is the main point for many of the other historical sites such as the 'Basilica Cistern' (an underground water system from 532 A.D., built by the Byzantine emperor Justinian. The cistern stored millions of gallons of water, brought from outside the city by an aqueduct. It was so well constructed; the cistern was used by the palace (including the Ottomans) for centuries. Walk through a maze of massive columns, reflected in clear pools of water (there are wooden boardwalks so you won't get your feet wet). The Hagia Sophia, (Church of the

Adventure: History + Culture
Destination: Istanbul

Holy Wisdom), completed by Justinian in 537 A.D., was the most celebrated building in Christian Byzantium. The interior of its huge dome, 184 ft high (taller than the Parthenon), was covered with glittering mosaics. In 1204, Crusaders looted the gold and silver icons from the church. When Constantinople fell to the Ottoman Turks, Aya Sofya became a mosque, and four minarets were added. Today, this magnificent building is a museum.

A stop at the stunning 'Grand Bazaar' (located at Bazaar Quarter) to pick up some Turkish delights is a must. This place is a shopaholics dream, whether you are after a carpet, silk slippers or tea you won't be disappointed. It is very easy to get lost here (so take care if you have young children) as the area covers a massive 307,000 metres squared and 22 gated entrances, yet everyday it is opened by 30,000 traders who are willing to haggle for your cash.

A trip to Istanbul wouldn't be complete without experiencing a traditional Turkish bath or hamam. A short tram or long walk away from Sultanahmet is the ancient 'Cermberlitas Baths'. It is a perfect way to recuperate from the overdose of sightseeing. Steam your aching muscles, scrub down your skin, and feel revived with a famous massage. The hamam was adopted by Islamic invaders who really did believe that cleanliness is next to Godliness, the bath was a chance to cleanse the skin but also restore the spirit. The hamam is still used today by Turks, but is obviously very popular with tourists and photographers – children over the age of 14 can use the baths, but be aware there are separate male and female sections.

There are other top attractions in the city for young and old children, such as 'Miniaturk'. It packs all of Turkey's most important buildings into one beautiful park, on the edge of the Golden Horn, it includes a miniature railway, model cars, boats, a cinema a maze and playground. And the 'Istanbul Toy museum', which is one of Istanbul's newest museums with around 4000 exhibits from rag dolls to a wild west gallery. This museum, placed in an old mansion (it once belonged to a wealthy family), is located in Goztepe area. The mansion is literally filled with old toys of all world countries and nations. The history of the museum is no less interesting than the exhibits. Quite recently, in 2005, the Turkish poet Sunay Akin has opened a private museum of toys in his family wooden house. Here are horses and dogs, robots and toy soldiers, dolls and houses. Theatre Hall also works as a theatre - puppet shows are given every week for 70 spectators. Finally, the Galata Tower, which is a cylindrical 62 metre former watchtower, is fun to climb (but there is a lift if children have tired feet), the views from the top are amazing. It has survived many earthquakes and there are 11 floors. In the evening the restaurant on the top floor hosts a dinner with cabaret Turkish folk dance and belly dancing.

Children definitely won't go hungry in Istanbul, with a 'sweetcorn' stand on every corner, and snacks such as 'simit', (which is a kind of giant pretzel with sesame), and Turkish Delights candy (lokum), flavoured with rosewater, lemon, cinnamon or mint in nearly every store.

Places to Stay

Neorion Hotel

Situated on the doorstep of most of the city sights. The boutique hotel of 58 rooms and suites is cosy and friendly. The swimming pool, Turkish bath, massage spa, cultural library, and museum-quality decorative arts are supplemented with complimentary fine arts musical performances, cuisine demonstrations and cultural events exclusively for hotel guests.

Guide Price: From £86 prpn
Best Room: Triple room for families

Çıragan Palace Kempinski

Perfect location for families visiting the city for short or long stay. The stunning palace of the late Ottoman period is situated quite literally on the shores of the Bosphorus, within walking distance to nearby Ortakoy, and a short taxi ride from Sultanahmet square. The rooms are generous and there is nice small children's play area and swimming pool for cooling off in the summer, and during every afternoon they serve the most delectable afternoon tea. For families who really want to arrive in style the hotel offers limousine or helicopter transfers from the airport.

Guide Price: From £220 prpn
Best Room: Lale Suite with kitchenette and dining table for 4 people

Hotel Les Ottomans

For swish families with older children head to this fine, new hip hotel. Built inside an Ottoman yali (a luxurious wooden mansion), the interior and 12 luxurious suites are decked out in lavish Ottoman style. The outdoor pool has a transparent floor panel that doubles as a spectacular ceiling in the swish subterranean spas.

Guide Price: From £500
Best Room: Turhan Hatice Suite

Places to Eat

Tere Kebab, Çengelköy

Situated directly on the Bosphorus River, with stunning views and a private water taxi to ferry you across. This stunning, yet local Turkish kebab house is popular with locals, and famed for their range of meat 'meze' dishes and excellent wines. As it is located on the residential Asian side it can be a bit of a mission to reach – but the quality food, and service make up for it.

360, Taksim

The city's smart, multiple award-winning eatery with a glass-walled rooftop extravaganza and a popular bar and a circular view of the metropolis. The culinary influences hail from all around the world, and dishes include delicious Lebanese kibbe meatballs stuffed with walnuts, veal-and-prawn surf and turf or lamb loin confit, expertly poached in olive oil for five whole hours. Not for young children.

Asitane, Edirnekapi

Asitane Restaurant is located in Edirnekapi, considered by many to be one of the most important areas of historical Istanbul. The chefs at Asitane scoured the archives for Sultans' festival menus at the Topkapi Palace kitchen, and recreated recipes from the 15th to the 18th centuries. Stuffed melon, or stuffed quince in winter, are to die for.

Opposite page from top. Valley of the chimneys, Cappadocia. Horse Riding in Cappadocia.

Focus On...
Cappadocia

A destination which should definitely not be missed is a visit to Cappadocia - an incredible land of strange rock formations and cave dwellings. You can hop aboard the sleeper train from Istanbul to Ankara or Konya then a relatively short bus ride to Goréme in Cappadocia, the journey itself is fun especially for children.

The surrealistic landscape of Cappadocia, is a strange area of multi-hued volcanic rock pillars and tortuous valleys sculpted by millennia of rain and wind, was first refuge for early Christians fleeing prosecution, and in Byzantine times became a vast complex of churches and monasteries, hollowed out of malleable rock, and adorned with frescoes depicting biblical scenes and saints. The underground cities of Derinkuyu and Kaymaklı, hollowed like the churches out of the volcanic rock and delving seven to nine floors into the earth, are a labyrinth of corridors, chambers, storerooms, kitchens and churches. The underground city at Derinkuyu has all the usual amenities found in other underground complexes across Cappadocia, such as wine and oil presses, stables, cellars, storage rooms, refectories, and chapels. Unique to the Derinkuyu underground city complex and located on the second floor is a spacious room with a barrel vaulted ceiling. It has been reported that this room was used as a religious school and the rooms to the left were studies. Between the third and fourth levels is a vertical staircase. This passage way leads to a cruciform church on the lowest level. Derinkuyu is by no means the only such city you can visit here. There are actually 40 or so subterranean settlements in the area although only a few are open to the public.

Above ground there is plenty to explore. The town of Avanos is famous for its beautiful old houses, pottery and onyx and no trip to Cappadocia would be complete without an overnight stay in a cave. The soft volcanic rock has been hollowed out for homes for at least two millennia. Recently, Cappadocia's enterprising hoteliers have restored crumbling stone-and-cave houses, equipped the rooms with comforts such as electricity, modern bathrooms, telephones, and even fast Internet connections, and opened them as traditional Cappadocian inns. Esbelli Evi ('the Esbelli House') is among the finest inns in Turkey—and it's in a cave. Every suite is tastefully decorated with antiques and crafts: Turkish carpets, brass or cast-iron king-size bedsteads, old lamps. Each suite has one or two bedrooms, (perfect for families) a living room or sitting area, kitchenette stocked with drinks, spacious bathroom and its own garden terrace area. An elaborate Turkish breakfast is included in the rate, with a selection of fruits, breads, cakes, breakfast cereals, yogurt, and over a dozen varieties of eggs and omelettes made to order.

Probably one of the other major highlights above ground is taking a half day excursion in a hot air balloon over the region. There are plenty of local companies who offer this, although depending somewhat on weather, if you catch a good clear day the views over the valleys can be mesmerizing, and the experience unforgettable for children.

ⓘ Stylish Essentials

General Information
Turkey Tourist Information
www.goturkey.com
Turkish Consulate
Rutland Lodge Rutland Gardens,
Knightsbridge
London SW7 1BW,
United Kingdom
www.turkishconsulate.org.uk
T. +44 (0) 20 7591 6900
(UK Enquiries)
E. consulate.london@mfa.gov.tr

Airlines
Turkish Airlines
www.turkishairlines.com
T. +90 (0) 212 444 0 849
(24 hour reservation)
British Airways
www.ba.com
T. 0844 493 0787
(UK reservation & enquiries)
Pegasus Airlines
www.flypgs.com/en
T. +90 (0) 212 371 55 00
(call centre)
EasyJet
www.easyjet.com
Jet2
www.jet2.com

Train Travel
TCDD
(Türkiye Cumhuryeti Devlet
Demiryollan)
www.tcdd.gov.tr
Rail Planner
www.turkeytravelplanner.com

Ionian Coast
Bodrum Tourist information
www.bodrum.org
Izmir Tourist Information
www.izmir.com
The Mausoleum at Halicarnassus
www.unmuseum.org/maus.htm
**The Bodrum Museum of
Underwater Archaeology**
www.bodrum-museum.com
T. +90 (0) 252 316 25 16

Gulet Sailing
www.bluecruise.org
4 Reasons Hotel
Yalikavak, P.K 46
Bodrum
www.4reasonshotel.com
T. +90 (0) 252 385 3212
E. info@4reasonshotel.com
Kempinski Hotel Barbaros Bay
Kızılagaç Köyü Gerenkuyu Mevkii
Yalıçiftlik, 48400 Bodrum
www.kempinski.com
T. +90 (0) 252 311 0303
Amanruya
Bülent Ecevit Cad.,
Demir Mevkii,
Göltürkbükü,
TR-48483 Bodrum, Turkey
www.amanresorts.com
T. +90 (0) 252 311 12 12
E. amanruya@amanresorts.com
Mezza Luna Izmir
Konak Pier
Ataturk Cad. No: 19, Izmir Konak Pier
www.mezzalunaizmir.com
T. +90 (0) 232 489 69 44
Otantik Ocakbasi
ataturk cad. kumbahce mah,
Bodrum
www.otantikocakbasi.com
T. +90 (0) 252 313 06 88
Maça Kizi Restaurant
www.macakizi.com
T. +90 (0) 252 377 62 72

Lycian Coast
RYA
www.rya.org.uk
T. +44 (0) 23 8060 4100
Learning to Sail
Göcek
www.nautilusyachting.com
T. +44 (0) 1732 867445
E. charter@nautilusyachting.com
Aspendos Opera & Ballet Festival
www.aspendosfestival.gov.tr
T. + 90 (0) 312 231 85 15
E. info@aspendosfestival.gov.tr

Dalya Life Retreat
Serefler köyü Tersakan
Mahallesi No:37 P.K:36
Dalaman-Göcek
www.Göcekotel.com
E. info@dalyalife.com
Hotel Villa Mahal
P.K 4 Kalkan
07960 Antalya
www.villamahal.com
E. info@villamahal.com
Deniz Feneri Lighthouse
Çukurba Yarim Adasi,
Beyhan Cenkçi Caddesi,
07580 Kas, Antalya.
www.exclusiveescapes.co.uk
Kalkan Aubergine
Kalkan Harbour No: 25-27
Kalkan Kas Antalya
www.kalkanaubergine.com
T. +90 (0) 242 844 3332
7 Mehmet
Muratpasa Dumlupınar Bulv.
201, 07333 Antalya
www.7mehmet.com
T. +90 (0)242 238 5200
Chez Evi
Telvi Sok. 4,
Kas
T. + 90 (0) 242 836-1253
Open 19.00–0.00

Istanbul
Topkapi Palace
Babihumayun Cad
Istanbul
www.topkapisarayi.gov.tr
T. +90 (0) 212 512 0480
Open Wednesday to Monday
9.00–17.00
Hagia Sophia
Sultanahmet Meydani
T. +90 (0) 212 528 4500
Open Tuesday to Sunday 9.00–19.00
Blue Mosque
Sultanahmet Meydani
T. +90 (0) 212 518 1319
Open daily 9.00–19.00, except
during prayers
Grand Bazaar
www.kapalicarsi.org.tr

Cermberlitas Baths
Vezir Hani Cad 8
www.cemberlitashamami.com.tr
T.+90 (0) 212 522 7974

Miniaturk
Horn Quarter, Imrahor Street
34445 Horn - Beyoglu
www.miniaturk.com.tr
T. +90 (0) 28 82 0212222

Istanbul Toy Museum
Ömerpasa Cad, Dr Zeki Zeren Sok
17, Göztepe
www.istanbuloyuncakmuzesi.com
T. +90 (0)216359 45 50/1
Open Tuesday to Friday 9.30–18.00,
Saturday to Sunday 9.30–19.00

Neorion Hotel
Orhaniye Street, No: 14 Sirkeci,
Istanbul
34110
T. +90 (0) 212 527 9090
E. info@neorionhotel.com

Hotel Les Ottomans
www.lesottomans.com
T. + 90 (0) 212 287 1024

Çıragan Palace Kempinski
Yıldız Mh. Çıragan Caddesi 32,
Istanbul
www.kempinski.com
T. +90 (0) 212 326 4646

Tere Kebab
Kuleli Caddesi No:53
Rıhtım Kat
Çengelköy
Istanbul
www.tere.com.tr
T. +90 (0) 216 422 5703
E. info@tere.com.tr

360
www.360istanbul.com
T. +90 (0) 212 251 10 42

Asitane
Kariye Camii Sok. 18,
Edirnekapi
T. +90 (0) 212 534 8414

Cappadocia

Cappadocia Information
www.cappadociaturkey.net

Hot Air Ballooning

Goreme Balloons
www.goremeballoons.com
T. +90 (384) 341 56 62
E. info@goremeballoons.com

Ballooning
www.hotairballooncappadocia.com
E. info@hotairballooncappadocia.com

Esbelli Evi
Esbelli Sokak, 8
50400 Ürgüp
Cappadocia
www.esbelli.com
T. +90 (0) 384 341 3395
E. esbelli@esbelli.com

Llamas, Peru.

PERU

Lima | Cusco & Machu Picchu |
Lake Titicaca | Arequipa

Columbia
Ecuador
Brazil
Lima ★
Machu Picchu
● Cusco
Bolivia
Pacific Ocean
Arequipa ●
Lake Titicaca
Chile

🏆 Why is this place so special?

Clinging to the Andes, between the desert and the expanse of the Amazon rainforest, Peru is an incredible country which offers such a wide range of family experiences that it can often be overwhelming. Exploring the ancient ruins of the Incas, discovering the lakes by boat, learning to surf, or visiting the labyrinthine of cities – there is something for everyone. Children will simply be mesmerised by the Peruvian culture, and will enjoy learning about the fascinating Inca history, and adrenaline junkies will fall at their feet with tiredness due to the range of exciting outdoor experiences, such as mountain biking, hiking and river rafting. Peru is not an easy destination for young babies and toddlers, but for juniors and teenagers, this would be a travel experience of a lifetime.

While Peru inevitably evokes images of Machu Picchu and the Inca empire, the country is also riddled with archaeological sites, and stunning museums showcasing this great civilization. Lima, which was announced a world cultural heritage site in 1991, is the country's capital, and often, the first point of entry into Peru. It is a vibrant, cosmopolitan metropolis steeped in vice-regal airs, and is the perfect starting point for travellers keen to experience Peru.

For many the highlight of Peru is travelling through the Andes to the old Inca capital, Cusco, which is a pleasant, lively place for families to explore, nearby there are ruined fortresses and Pisac's bustling and colourful markets. From Cusco, families can catch the scenic luxurious Hiram Bingham train up to Machu Picchu (or hike up a different route), marvel at the 'lost city' and its stunning jungle backdrop, and even spend the night on the world heritage site itself.

From Machu Picchu, families can explore the floating Uros islands on Lake Titicaca. Standing at over 12,000 feet, Titicaca is one of the highest navigable lakes in the world, and there are pre-Incan Uros who live on a series of floating islands. Only a few hundred

Uros remain on the islands, as thousands of others have moved to the mainland, which means that a trip and an overnight stay with these villagers, makes this experience all the more special.

No trip to Peru would be complete without seeing a llama or an Alpaca. Children will adore these social, curious and fluffy animals. Incas were the original domesticators of llamas and alpacas, and this occurred in the higher Andes Mountains around 4,000 B.C., they are an important aspect of Inca life, supplying wool for clothing. You can visit many llama or Alpaca farms throughout Peru, especially near Lake Titicaca or the sacred valley.

Arequipa, the second largest city in Peru, is situated along the south-west, and was declared a world cultural heritage site in 2000. The city itself is known as the 'White City' because it is mainly built out of the volcanic rock or sillar. The city is where visitors can see a fascinating display of mummies, preserved in ice and discovered high in the Andes. As well as the colonial architecture and dormant volcanoes, the region is also home to unblemished beaches with white sand, blue sea and with bright sunshine most of the year, makes a great spot for relaxation for a few days.

📖 Fun Facts

Capital: Lima.

Population: 28,302,603.

Currency: Nuevo Sol (S/.).

Languages: Spanish & Quechua.

Trivia: Out of a total of 32 different kinds of climates found here on Earth, Peru has 28 of them, including dense rainforest, icy mountains, humid savannas, cold plateaus, dry forests, and hot plateaus.

Getting there and exploring around

Peru has many flights linked up with North America, the UK and Europe, Australia and New Zealand, Asia and Africa, as well as the rest of Latin America. Many South American capitals have direct flights to Lima, and there are economical 'South American' air passes available if you are planning on spending time elsewhere. If you're headed to Cusco, and flying to Peru from another continent, your flight will most likely land in Lima first, during the late afternoon or evening, meaning you'll have to wait until morning to catch the next flight to Cusco (something to bear in mind with tired children). Some of the best deals for travellers visiting many countries on different continents are Round-the-World (RTW) tickets. Itineraries from the USA, Europe or Australasia typically require at least five stopovers, possibly including unusual destinations such as Tahiti or South American cities.

Arriving in Peru is typically a straightforward process, as long as your passport is valid for at least six months beyond your departure date. When arriving by air, US citizens must show a return ticket or open-jaw onward ticket – don't show up with just a one-way ticket to South America. When arriving by air or overland, immigration officials may only stamp 30 days into your passport (though 90 days is standard); if this happens, explain how many more days you need, supported by an exit ticket for onward or return travel.

Several overseas companies offer tours around Peru for travellers who have a limited amount of time. Usually, groups travel with knowledgeable guides, but you will pay a great deal extra for this privilege – it's worth it for highly specialized outdoor activities (i.e. river running, mountaineering). Otherwise, it's just as convenient and much cheaper to travel to Peru independently, and then take organized day trips and overnight tours along the way.

Best time of year to visit

Peru's climate has two main seasons – wet and dry – though the weather varies greatly depending on the geographical region. Temperature is mostly influenced by elevation: the higher you climb, the cooler it becomes.

The peak tourist season runs from June to August, which coincides with the cooler dry season in the Andean highlands and the summer holidays in North America and Europe. This is the best (and busiest) time to go trekking on the Inca Trail to Machu Picchu, or climbing, hiking and mountain biking elsewhere.

On the arid coast, Peruvians visit the beaches during the most hot and humid time of the year, from late December through March. In central and southern Peru, the coast is cloaked in garúa (coastal fog) for the rest of the year. Although the southern beaches are deserted then, the coastal cities can be visited at any time. In the north, the coast usually sees more sun, so beach lovers can hang out there year-round.

? Must know before you go

Trekking essentials. Most trekking expeditions suggestion a minimum age of 12 year old, as the hikes can be demanding, and expect to walk on average 5-7 hours per day, so make sure the family are fit enough before travelling. It can get cold at night in the Andes, so take plenty of warm clothing. In the mountains, the altitude doesn't seem to cause children as many problems as it does for adults, but they shouldn't walk too hard above 2000m without full acclimatisation.

Learn the lingo. Learning a few words in Spanish will go along way to enjoying the experience of Peru. Whilst most tourist areas, such as in Lima, hoteliers will speak some English, if you are travelling to areas off-the-beaten track, then a basic grasp of Spanish is a must.

Short on time? If you have only 7 or 10 days to experience Peru, then it might make sense to book your trip with an organised adventure company, rather an independently. This means that they will plan your itinerary with plenty of activities, accommodation and guide-led experiences. Booking as part of a 'tour group', might not necessarily mean top-end accommodation but it will be fun for children as they will get to meet and make friends with others.

📖 Highlights

History in Lima. Spend a day or two exploring the Museo de la Nacion, visiting the colonial centre (based around the Plaza de Armas) and monastery of Santo Domingo.

Overnight on Machu Picchu. Take the luxury 'Hiram Bingham' train to Machu Picchu and spend a night at Sanctuary Lodge

Local Life on the Lake. Travel by boat to the floating Uros islands at Lake Titicaca and observe local life

Arequipa Legends. Visit the fascinating display of mummies on ice, and listen to the legend of Juanita.

FUN FAMILY FACT:
Most Peruvians actually go through 2 marriages, the civil and the religious. Within ancient Incan custom, couples were not considered properly married unless they exchanged their sandals!

 Tip for the Trip

"Don't force feed culture. A day or two exploring museums and architecture may be more than enough for teenagers, and then boredom sets in. In some cases education occurs in the ways you don't expect it, children don't need to have their head in museums to be able to understand and appreciate culture – this can be experienced in more ways, such as, people watching from a café or taking photos of locals."

Adventure: History + Culture
Destination: Lima

✦ Regional Information

Peru's capital Lima is a vibrant, cosmopolitan city that embraces its colonial heritage, modern dynamism, and privileged location on the Pacific coast. The city is, after all, the only South American capital facing the sea. As well as its cultural heritage, Lima has become recognized as one of the world's top gastronomic destinations, as the city's vibrant and creative coastal fusion cuisine has gained in fame worldwide. Spending a night or two in Lima makes a great introduction to the rest of Peru. It also helps to break up the long journey for children, especially if you have been travelling from another continent.

Only a few years ago, Lima was not often viewed as a significant tourist destination on its own, but that image has changed, perhaps due to the gastronomic boom that has accompanied solid economic progress and increased safety in the capital. Lima's magnificent collection of art and archaeology museums, the finest in Peru, as well as the well preserved colonial centre and lively contemporary communities like Miraflores, San Isidro and Barranco hugging the coast, make Lima a fascinating place that takes at least two days to discover and appreciate.

The historical centre of Lima conserves numerous constructions, that due to its immense beauty, in the architectural context, was declared as 'World Heritage Site' by UNESCO. Independently the Church and Convent of San Francisco were also declared Cultural World Heritage Sites. The centre of the colonial city of Lima is the Plaza de Armas, and is the site at which Francisco Pizarro (conquistador who eradicated the Inca Empire) founded the city in 1535, hence the naming of the Convent. The fountain in the centre, however, is one of the few things that date back to before the earthquake. If you plan to visit the centre of Lima, be sure to arrive in the square at 12pm sharp, where in the forecourt of the Palacio you will see the changing of the guard. The building on the fourth side of the square is La Cathedral which was the first building to be reconstructed after the earthquake making it the oldest on the square.

Adventure: History + Culture
Destination: Lima

There are several good museums in Lima, but the 'Museo de la Nacion' is a good introduction to the archaeological sites you may be visiting later around Peru. Inaugurated in 1990, there are exhibitions in big rooms distributed in four levels, with a sample that recreates all the pre-Hispanic manifestations among 14,000 B.C. and 1532 A.D. Ceramic exhibition, replicas of the main archaeological places of Peru. Dioramas, paintings and diverse collections that represent the different aspects of the development of the old Peru. Restoration shops, historical file, libraries, galleries and auditorium. Interesting also is the 'Museo Nacional de la Cultura Peruana', which was founded in 1946, and exhibiting popular Peruvian arts, amazon and folkloric ethnology; fabrics, ceramic, musical instruments, imagery, etc.

Finally, the Gold museum (Museo de Oro del Peru) is also particularly interesting for children, featuring over six thousand gold relics, thousands of years old - although some are replicas and not the real thing, it is still a museum must-see. Children's' eyes will literally glaze over with daydreams of Indiana Jones-type adventures. If you only have time for one museum, this is the one.

Once you've covered all the museums head to Barranco, the suburb next to Miraflores, which has great sea views and little food and craft stalls. It has a very relaxed, bohemian atmosphere, with painted art-deco houses and even free public dance classes in the 'Parque Principal'. To let off energy, there are a few green spaces around Miraflores, such as the 'Parque de la Amistad' (Santiago de Surco), which has a miniature steam train, and typical Andean train station, artificial lake, lots of grass to run around. There is also the 'Parque Kennedy' a pleasant park which has swings, slides, and an excellent playground. Around the park there are several cafes where you can find snacks.

Places to Stay

DUO Hotel Boutique

A small hotel with just 20 rooms and suites, located in the district of San Isidro, offering a calm environment for travellers. It's located only 2 blocks away from San Isidro golf club, and has a warm homely feel.

Guide Price: From £69 prpn
Best Room: DUO suite is a mini duplex apartment style

Casa Andina Miraflores

A small luxury hotel located in Miraflores, just 2 blocks from Park Kennedy and surrounded by Lima's finest dining and shopping areas. These 148 Lima accommodations are divided into Traditional and Superior rooms, as well as Suites, Senior Suites and a grand Imperial Suite, all decorated with Peruvian artwork selected by curators of the renowned Larco Museum. There is also a covered heated pool with an open air terrace.

Guide Price: From £118 prpn
Best Room: Suite with a separate sitting area which can be used as a make-up bed

Miraflores Park Hotel

One of Lima's fine luxury hotels with a superb spa and roof-top swimming pool, in a beautiful setting overlooking the Pacific Ocean. It is close to the historical sites, and just a block and half away is the Larcomar Entertainment Centre, Lima's largest mall, where you'll find world-class shopping, dining and entertainment.

Guide Price: From £150 prpn
Best Room: Junior suite, large enough for 2 adults and 2 children

Places to Eat

Pescados Capitales, Miraflores

One of Lima's best cevicheria. The menus is massive, offering every type of fish, an a nice array of classic cevicheria starters like Tequeños Capitales –fried triangular wantans stuffed with shrimp and egg – and Conchitas a la Chalaca – scallops in the shell with a splash of lime, red onion, tomato, and ají. For simple palates, there are grilled options, such as Salmon, Tuna, Sea Bass, and Swordfish, as well as Sole, and it's not over pricey either making it a good lunch of evening meal option.

Restaurant Huaca Pucllana, Miraflores

This great restaurant is located in a breathtaking setting: within the ruins of an archaeological compound built between 200 and 700 A.D. by the early inhabitants of Lima. Their cuisine is a reinterpretation of Peruvian Criollo tradition, and features such dishes as ceviche de camarones a la piedra (stone prawn ceviche) and locro de costillas de cordero (lamb-ribs with a pumpkin stew).

Astrid & Gastón, Lima

Founded in 1994 by husband-and-wife couple Gastón Acurio and Astrid Gutsche, initially the restaurant's cuisine was largely French. Gradually, though, as they rediscovered Peruvian flavours and culinary traditions, the kitchen began to incorporate local dishes and ingredients, moving towards the current Criollo-French concept that characterizes the restaurant today. In any case, regardless of this evolution -or precisely because of it-, consider Astrid & Gastón one of the highest notes in the Peruvian culinary scene.

Adventure:
Action + Adventure
Destination: Cusco +
Machu Picchu

✦ **Regional Information**

The city of Cusco, declared a World Cultural Heritage by UNESCO in 1983, which in the ancient Quechua language means 'navel of the world', was an important hub in Inca times that connected all of South America, from Colombia to the north of Argentina. Today, centuries later, Cusco continues to be the centre of attention, not only for our neighbouring countries but for the whole world. In its streets, historical centres, churches, pubs and cafés you can hear not only Quechua and Spanish spoken, but such diverse languages as English, French, Japanese and Hebrew. All of them, united by the same experience, found in the charming and fascinating 'belly button' of the world.

Cusco also carries the title of the archaeological capital of South America with pride, because there is no other place in the whole continent where you can easily reach ruins of amazing culture, which are still in a good condition. It is surrounded by six mountains; some more than 6,000 metres high, as well as being the oldest city in the western hemisphere and the cradle of the ancient Inca civilization. And, of course, it is known all over the world for its proximity to the amazing archaeological ruins of Machu Picchu, it is often the starting point for trips up to Machu Picchu, and many chose to stay a day or two in Cusco.

Machu Picchu, the Lost City of the Incas, is one of the most famous examples of Inca architecture and is located 112 kilometres from Cusco (a 3½ hour train journey), 2,350 metres above sea level. The ruins are located in a lush jungle and are believed to have been built in the mid-15th century by Inca Pachacutec. Lost in history, the ruins were not discovered until 1911 by the American explorer, Hiram Bingham. This famous citadel combines the visual and spiritual force of magnificent natural scenery with the natural diversity of a historic sanctuary, recognised as a Cultural and Natural Patrimony of the World. Only the Inca and his noblemen, priests, priestesses and chosen women (Akllas) had free access to the premises of the Machu Picchu sanctuary.

Opposite page. Left. Machu Picchu
Sanctuary Lodge © Orient-Express Hotels
(UK) Ltd and Genivs Loci.
Right. Alpaca Carpaccio, Cusco.

Adventure: Action + Adventure
Destination: Cusco + Machu Picchu

We can only admire the Incas for what they did - they literally flattened the top of a high mountain to build a city comprising of hundreds of buildings with an agricultural production area, irrigation system and other facilities. The rock cutting and shaping, the dry stone techniques (assembling huge bricks without mortar) used for constructing the buildings of Machu Picchu are still a mystery and only speculations exist about how this could have been done.

With the right information, getting to Machu Picchu shouldn't be as much a mystery as the place itself. You can either book all the components of the trip yourself or you can buy a ready made package tour from one of hundreds of tour operators offering this service. However as Machu Picchu becomes more and more of a popular destination it is important to try and make your arrangements as far in advance as you can, especially as the government have recently limited the number of tourists per day.

Visiting Machu Picchu is possible by hiking in the Andean Mountains along the Inca Trail or by combining train and bus transportation all the way up to the site. The most exciting way, however, is to get there through the Andes. The classic 4 day Inca trail is adventurous and fun for families and you'll get to see other wonderful sights, such as Runkuracay, Llactapata, and Huinay Huayna along the way.

There are hundreds of tour companies in Cusco and Lima queuing up to sell you a space on their tours to Machu Picchu, as well as specialist (and not so specialist) international tour operators. Most local operators offer a simple one day excursion from Cusco to Machu Picchu including all transport and a professional guide (check to see if the guide speaks good English). It is also worth checking to see what the maximum number of people in the group is before travelling.

Families wanting a more luxurious experience can travel to Machu Picchu without the hike. The Hiram Bingham train is the most indulgent way to journey between Cusco and Machu Picchu. The Hiram Bingham is named after the previously mentioned explorer. The carriages are painted a distinctive blue and gold and the interiors are luxurious, warm and inviting with elegant decoration in the style of the 1920's Pullman trains. As passengers step on board they are surrounded by a world of polished wood, gleaming cutlery and glittering crystal. The train is composed of two dining cars, an observation bar car and a kitchen car, and can carry up to 84 passengers. Peru Rail also offer a variety of other train services for those not wanting to climb or to spend money, such as the 'backpacker' service, which allows large backpacks to be stored above comfortable seats.

For many the highlight of a trip to Peru is seeing 'Machu Picchu' itself, so it is worth certainly spend a night here to experience the wonder without the hoards of tourists.

Place to Stay

Places to Eat

Casa Andina Private Collection - Cusco

A beautifully renovated 18th-century manor house, just 3 blocks from Cusco's Plaza de Armas, has an authentic colonial character. The hotel is distinguished by its 3 interior patios with wooden balconies. The principal patio, featuring a gurgling stone fountain, is one of Cusco's emblematic colonial courtyards, and oxygen rooms to help with acclimatisation to altitude.

Guide Price: From £170 prpn
Best Room: A suite with Oxygen

Hotel Monasterio Cusco

Built as a monastery in 1592, Hotel Monasterio retains the charm and ambience that has existed for centuries whilst boasting a reputation as one of the world's finest hotels. It has 126 rooms, many of them with charming views of the city, the colourful rooftops of Cusco or the beautiful inner courtyards of the hotel. They also offer Horseback riding, Paragliding, Whitewater rafting, and guided tours of Machu Picchu, and can arrange for the luxury train transfer to the Sanctuary Lodge, which is part of 'Orient-Express'.

Guide Price: From £350 prpn
Best Room: A Junior Suite on 2 levels, with Oxygen Enrichment

Machu Picchu Sanctuary Lodge

An Orient-Express hideaway - Machu Picchu Sanctuary Lodge is the only hotel located adjacent to this ancient Inca citadel. It offers its guests exceptionally easy access from early morning to late afternoon, when most of the day visitors and buses have left. If you can afford it, it is definitely worth it to splurge on a room here for just one night.

Guide Price: From £578 prpn
Best Room: Deluxe Twin Mountain View & Terrace

Limo Cocina Peruana Restaurant, Cusco

A well-regarded restaurant serving classic Peruvian fare, with a view over the main square, this restaurant is tucked upstairs and has a great atmosphere

Inca Grill, Cusco

Inca Grill offers the best food in town and although a tad expensive. The menu includes a wide range of typical and international dishes including vegetarian dishes. Elegant folk shows are put on each evening. Check out the 'Novo Sampler platter' with stuffed chili peppers, kiwicha chicken fingers, alpaca brochettes, and quinoa croquettes. Reservations are a good idea.

Cicciolina, Cusco

Nicely decorated, Spanish / Italian / Mediterranean cuisine, with beautifully presented tapas food. Nice atmosphere, sophisticated, (presented like a Spanish 'Bodega') if a little on the expensive side. Reservations are a must May to September.

Adventure: Nature + Wildlife
Destination: Lake Titicaca

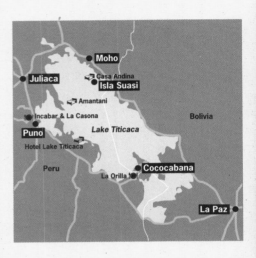

Regional Information

Lake Titicaca is the highest navigable lake on earth at 11,463 feet altitude. Straddling the border between Peru and Bolivia, the Andean peoples refer to the lake as 'The Sacred Lake': and legends say that the first Inca rose from its depths and went out to found the Inca Empire. Actually two lakes joined by the Strait of Tiquina, it sprawls over 3,500 square miles, fed by waters from the melting snows of the Andes.

Nearby, on the Bolivian side of the lake, arose the population and ceremonial centre of Tiahuanaco, capital of one of the most important civilizations of South America. Tiahuanaco ceremonial sites were built along the lake's shores, indicating that the lake was considered sacred at least 2,000 years ago.

Sitting in this turquoise lake are islands inhabited by people with disparate cultures that today combine their pre-Inca heritage with Inca and Spanish influences. Fishermen living on islands made of reeds, farmers carving terraces in rock-covered hillsides and shepherd herding flocks of llamas and alpacas - all consider the lake sacred and the source of life. Around the lake you can find signs of the past, from pre-Inca burial tombs to Spanish built cathedrals.

The flora and fauna is no less unique than the cultures found here. The tortora reed, a cat-tail type rush is used to build islands, buildings and boats. Llamas, alpacas and vicuñas are raised as food, beasts of burden and most importantly, for their fine wool used in textile weavings. One of the most unusual animals found here is the Lake Titicaca frog which is endemic to this seemingly hostile low temperature, high ultraviolet light environment. Its' skin looks several sizes too large, thereby giving it a large enough surface area for the frog to take enough oxygen from the water to allow to stay submerged and protected. All of this makes for a unique travel destination, and there are plenty of experiences in and around the lake for families, such as kayaking, horseback riding, or biking making it an indispensable part of any trip to Peru.

Adventure: Nature + Wildlife
Destination: Lake Titicaca

The most unique of the islands dotting on Titicaca's surface are the Uros. They are floating islands man-made of totora reeds. The islands (there are over 40 of them), are populated by hard living people, who survive by fishing and nowadays because of the increasing tourism. Their handcrafts are wonderful, and the people are very hospitable. The Uros, who fled to the middle of the lake to escape conflicts with the Collas and Incas, long ago began intermarrying with the Aymara Indians, and many have now converted to Catholicism. Fishers and birders, they live grouped by family sectors, and entire families live in one-room tent -like thatched huts constructed on the shifting reed island that floats beneath. Travellers might be surprised, to say the least, to find some huts outfitted with televisions powered by solar panels (which were donated by the Fujimori administration after a presidential visit to the islands). Incredibly, the Fujimori government also built some solar-powered aluminium houses on several islands, but few if any locals actually dwell in them, because they are very hot during the day and brutally cold at night. For a fee, locals will take visitors on short rides from one island to another in the reed boats, but you should consider it a contribution to the community.

Other islands include Taquile Island, which is a small narrow island with its main town up on a hill. Taquileños are known for their fine handwoven textiles and clothing. Travellers can buy well made woollen and alpaca goods as well as colourful garments whose patterns and designs bear hidden messages about the wearer's social standing or marital status. And also Amantani Island, which is a circular island of about 9 square miles, is inhabited by Aymara people. This is an agricultural community of six villages, and there are two sacred mountain peaks, Pachatata (Father Earth) and Pachamama (Mother Earth) divide the fields and the pastures for cattle, sheep, and the famous alpacas, and travellers can stay here with local families.

A traditional celebration of the Feast Day of Santiago is held here every July. If you are lucky enough to catch a festival on the island, you will be treated to a festive and stubbornly traditional pageant of colour, marked by picturesque dances and women twirling in circles, revealing as many as 16 layered, multicoloured skirts. Any time on the island, though, offers unique experiences – especially once the day-trippers have departed and you have the island and incomparable views of the blue waters framed by stone archways virtually to yourself. Taquile then seems about as far away from modernity and 'civilization' as one can travel on this planet.

The most convenient way to visit Titicaca is by an inexpensive and well-run guided tour, arranged by one of several travel agencies in Puno. Although it is possible to arrange independent travel, the low cost and easy organization of group travel don't encourage it. You can go on a half-day tour of the Uros Floating Islands or a full-day tour that includes Taquile Island, but the best way to experience Lake Titicaca's unique indigenous life is to stay at least 1 night on either Taquile or Amantaní. Those with more time and money to burn may want to explore the singular experience of staying on Private Isla Suasi, home to little more than a solar-powered hotel and a dozen llamas and vicuñas.

Places to Stay

Amantani Family Homestay

A chance to stay with the locals of Amantani is wonderful. It is basic but comfortable, and fun, especially for children. Your family will provide you with meals for dinner and breakfast and also show you the local sites as well as dress you up for the night time 'Inca Disco'. It is really a good way of giving back to the community. Take some groceries as a gift for your family and sit down with them and test your knowledge of 'quecha' the local dialect.

Best Room: N/A
Guide Price: Very cheap!

Casa Andina Private Collection - Isla Suasi

A solar powered eco-lodge on remote private island Suasi. Featuring panoramic lake views from every room, surrounded by terraced gardens and designed with native materials to blend into the island, the lodge is committed to being green. Rooms come with pressurised oxygen and chimneys, down comforters & hot water bottles to warm beds, for cold winter nights. They also offer nature walks, canoeing, boating and star-gazing excursions.

Best Room: The enormous Andean Cottage, 2 bed, 3 bathroom suite
Guide Price: From £200 prpn

Titilaka Lodge

Eighteen fully serviced lake-view suites feature heated floors and spa bathrooms, with large oversized tubs and massage showers. Here you will find a haven for re-energizing after a day of excursion by boat, mountain bike, hiking or car. All rooms have wonderful views of the immense lake.

Best Room: The 'Dusk' room, with two windows and two double beds

Guide Price: From £250 prpn

Places to Eat

La Orilla, Copacabana

Situated about 20m (66 ft.) from the beach, has a terrace that overlooks the lake. The trout curry is highly recommended. Other excellent options include a vegetable stir-fry, fajitas, and spring rolls. On the weekends, live bands sometimes perform here.

Incabar, Puno

Stylish and funky this lounge bar/restaurant aims high. The menu is much more creative and flavourful than other places in town (even if dishes don't always succeed), with interesting sauces for lake fish and alpaca steak, curries, and stir fries, and artful presentations.

La Casona, Puno

Puno's most distinguished eatery calls itself a 'museum-restaurant.' La Casona ('big house') has traditional, rather old-style Spanish charm, with lace tablecloths. The three dining rooms are filled with antiques, but it retains a decidedly informal appeal. Its specialty is Titicaca lake fish, such as trout and kingfish, served La Casona style, which means with a kitchen-sink preparation of rice, avocado, ham, cheese, hot dog, apple salad, french fries, and mushrooms. If you're here for dinner, ask about the menú del día, which is not advertised, but is usually a great deal.

Focus On...
Arequipa

Arequipa is well known for its glistening white buildings made from sillar, a white volcanic rock, which gives the city its nickname 'La Ciudad Blanca' or 'The White City'.

It is Peru's second largest city and was founded in 1540. The site was chosen for its proximity to the coast, enabling settlers to trade the products of Cusco and the mines of Potosi (Bolivia) with Lima. The local cultivation of wheat, corn and grapes all contributed to the regions economic growth. The city is surrounded by 3 volcanoes; El Misti, still active at 5822m, the higher and extinct Chachani 6075m and Pichu Pichu 5571m. The Incas highly respected these volcanoes since the melt water from their snow-capped peaks form the headwaters of the mighty Amazon River, thousands of kilometres away. It is worth a short stay here at the end of a Peruvian adventure, before heading back via Lima, if anything just to explore the 'Inca mummies', which children will find fascinating.

In spite of its interesting collection of mummies and artefacts from the Inca Empire, most visitors come to the 'Museo Santuarios Andinos' for the Dama de Ampato (the Ice Maiden of Ampato). 'Juanita', as it's more familiarly known, is an Inca mummy of a twelve to fourteen year old girl found atop the dormant Ampato volcano by the climber Miguel Zárate, the archaeologist José Chávez, and the anthropologist Johan Reinhard in 1995.

It is believed that 'Juanita' was the victim of a ritualistic sacrifice to the Gods (a violent blow to the temple, according to the studies) and buried in ice at 6,380m. Given that only Inca priests were allowed to ascend to such a high point, where the gods were believed live, it's probable that the sacrifice was committed by the priests themselves, some 500 years ago. It is important to note that the Ice Maiden of Ampato is not on exhibit from January to April each year, due to restoration.

Another one of Arequipa's leading attractions is the Plaza de Armas, and is one of the most beautiful squares in Peru. On the north side of the Plaza is the impressive, twin-towered Cathedral, founded in 1612 and largely rebuilt in the 19th Century having been repeatedly damaged by earthquakes and fire. The Plaza is surrounded on its other 3 sides by colonial arcaded buildings with many cafes and restaurants. Behind the Cathedral is a pretty back street with many handicraft shops.

Most people who visit Arequipa also take a tour out to the Cañon de Colca, one of the world's deepest canyons formed by an enormous seismic fault between the Coropuna (6425m) and Ampato (6325m) volcanoes. A tour can be arranged on arrival in Arequipa at one of the several tour operators or travel agents around the Plaza. Although a tour can be fit into one day, it's best to go for at least 2 days, staying the night at the village of Chivay the first village on the edge of the canyon. Remember to bring a swimming costume and towel for a visit to the thermal springs on the outskirts of Chivay.

(i) Stylish Essentials

General Information

Official Tourist Information
www.peru.travel

Foreign & Commonwealth Office Travel Advice
www.fco.gov.uk

Embassy of Peru
Visas, foreign affairs and
travel information
www.peruembassy-uk.com

Aerolineas Argentinas
T. + 44 (0) 800 0969 747
(UK reservations)
www.aerolineas.com.ar

Aeroméxico
www.aeromexico.com
T. + 80053407 (Peru call centre)

Aeropostal
Offices 501-02, Martir Olaya 129,
Miraflores
Lima
www.aeropostal.com
E. reservaciones@aeropostal.com

American Airlines
www.aa.com
T. +44 (0)844 499 7300
(UK reservations, Outside the US)
T. +1 800 433 7300 (Within the US)

British Airways
www.ba.com
T. +44 (0) 844 493 0787
(UK reservations & enquiries)

TACA
www.taca.com
T. +44 (0) 8702 410 340
(UK reservations)

Varig
www.varig.com

Rail Networks

Peru Rail
www.perurail.com
T. +51 (0) 84 581414
(Peru call centre)
E. reservas@perurail.com

Hiram Bingham
www.orient-express.com
T. +44 (0) 845 077 2222
(UK call centre)
E. oereservations.uk@orient-express.com

Inca Rail
105 Calle Portal de Panes
Plaza de Armas,
Cusco
www.incarail.com
T. +51 (0) 84 233030
(Cusco call centre)

Tour Companies

Active South America
www.activesouthamerica.com

The Adventure Company
Peru group itineraries & tours
for families
www.adventurecompany.co.uk

Responsible Travel
Living like a local, day trips and
organised tours
www.responsibletravel.com

Llama Travel
South America & Peru travel
specialists
www.llamatravel.com

Journey Latin America
Specialist in all things Latin America
www.journeylatinamerica.co.uk

Lima

Museo de la Nación
(Museum of the Nation)
Javier Prado Este Avenue No. 2465,
San Borja.
T. +51 (0) 1 476 9875
Open Tuesday to Sunday from
9.00–18.00

Museo Nacional de la Cultura Peruana (National Museum of the
Peruvian Culture)
Alfonso Ugarte Avenue No. 650,
Lima
T. + 51 (0) 1 423 5892
Open Tuesday to Saturday from
10.00–14.30

Museo de Oro del Peru
(Museum of Peruvian Gold)
Alonso De Molina,
Lima
www.museoroperu.com.pe
T. +51 (0) 1 435 0791

Parque Kennedy
Parque 7 de Junio, Parque Central
Miraflores,
Lima

DUO Hotel Boutique
F. Valle Riesta 576,
San Isidro, Lima 27
www.duohotelperu.com
T. +51 (0) 1 628 3245

Casa Andina Miraflores
Av La Paz 463
Miraflores,
Lima
www.casa-andina.com
T. +51 (0) 1 213 9739

Miraflores Park Hotel
Miraflores, Lima
www.mirafloorespark.com
T. +51 (0) 1610 4000

Pescados Capitales
La Mar 1337, Miraflores,
Lima
www.pescadoscapitales.com
T. +51 (0) 1 421 8808

Restaurant Huaca Pucllana
General Borgoño, Block 8 (Huaca
Pucllana),
Miraflores
www.resthuacapucllana.com
T. +51 (0) 1 445 4042

Astrid & Gaston
Calle cantuarias 175 Miraflores, Lima
www.astridygaston.com
T. +51 (0)1 242 5387

Cusco & Machu Picchu

Machu Picchu Trekking Company
Los Pinos St. 156 Of 502,
Miraflores, Lima 18.
www.machupicchutreks.com
T. +51 (1) 242 9716
E. info@machupicchutreks.com

Casa Andina Private Collection
Plazoleta Limacpampa Chico 473,
Cusco
www.casa-andina.com
T. +51 (0) 1 213 9739
E. travel@casa-andina.com

Hotel Monasterio
Calle Palacio 136,
Plazoleta Nazarenas,
Cusco
www.monasteriohotel.com
T. +51 (0) 84 60 4000
E. perures.fits@orient-express.com

Sanctuary Lodge Hotel
Monumento Arqueologico de Machu Picchu
Machu Picchu,
Cusco
www.sanctuarylodgehotel.com
T. +51 (0) 84 984 816 953
E. individuals.sanctuarylodge@
orient-express.com

Limo Cocina Peruana Restaurant
Cusco
Portal de Carnes 236, 2nd floor

Inca Grill
Portal de Panes 115,
Plaza de Armas
Cusco
www.inkagrillcusco.com
T. +51 (0) 26 29 92

Cicciolina
Calle Triunfo 393, 2nd floor
Cusco
www.cicciolinacuzco.com

Lake Titicaca

General Information
www.laketiticaca.org

Adventures & Experiences
Lake Titicaca (inc homestay)
www.edgaradventures.com

Titilaka Lodge
Puno
www.titilaka.com
T. +51 (0) 1 7005111

Casa Andina Private Collection - Isla Suasi
Isla Suasi, Puno
www.casa-andina.com
T. +51 (0) 1 213 9739
E. travel@casa-andina.com

La Orilla
Av. 6 de Agosto
Copacabana
Lake Titicaca

Incabar
Jr. Lima 348,
Puno
T. +51 (0) 51 368 031

La Casona
Jr. Lima 517,
Puno
T. + 51 (0) 51 351 108

Arequipa

Arequipa Tourist Information
www.aboutarequipa.com

Museo Santuarios Andinos
La Merced 110,
Arequipa
www.ucsm.edu.pe/santury/
E. santury@ucsm.edu.pe

Cañon de Colca
Tourist Information
www.colca.info

Sonesta Posadas Del Inca Arequipa Portal de Flores
116 Arequipa, Peru
www.sonesta.com/Arequipa
T. +51 (0) 54 21.55 30

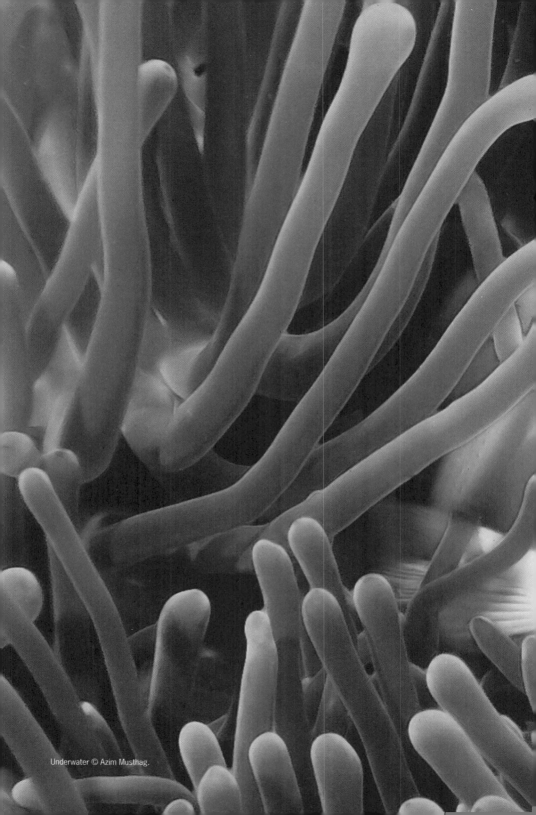

Underwater © Azim Musthag.

MALDIVES

North Malé Atoll | Haa Alif Atoll |
South Malé Atoll | Malé

MALDIVES

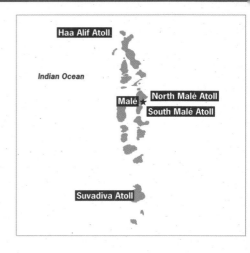

Haa Alif Atoll

Indian Ocean

Malé
North Malé Atoll
South Malé Atoll

Suvadiva Atoll

🏆 Why is this place so special?

The Maldives consists of approximately 1,190 coral islands and a chain of 26 atolls which are scattered along the north and south direction, and only 1% of this surface is land. So it is relatively small in terms of land mass and also population, but the island nation is mighty in terms of remarkable (and luxurious) experiences for travellers. The Maldives has been readily identified as a 'honeymoon hotspot' and rightly so, offering sunshine, unspoiled islands of sand and butler-led resorts. However, for families, (especially those with young children and toddlers) it can make a memorable, exciting, and even relaxing trip of a lifetime – if you can survive the long haul flight.

Most travellers head to the Maldives for the pristine, powder white beaches. And they are rarely disappointed. Having bounced back from a series of natural disasters in the past few years including the coral bleaching by El Niño and the horror of the 2004 tsunami. Its beaches are superior to anywhere in the world, and the sea is so warm (like bath water), it is a country that has become a byword for paradise be it for sun worshippers, divers, snorkelers or surfers. The beaches are also relatively safe, and with shallow waters lapping each island, it's easy swimming even for babies and toddlers. Tourism is also carefully regulated, with close regard paid to the natural environment, and resorts are of a universally high standard (which is reassuring for families) with excellent facilities, and an abundance of things to do.

The early history of the Maldives may be shrouded in mystery but its more recent past is readily documented. Like nations nearby, Sultans and Colonial powers played a strong hand in shaping the country's past but the 1,400 year-long Buddhist Kingdom shaped the people most. And while the local traditions are difficult to experience on a resort atoll, a trip to a local village or Malé (the capital) can easily make a journey here a whole different experience.

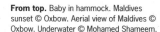

The chain of atolls, which are ring-shaped coral reefs with a lagoon centre, is a borrowing from the Maldivian language 'Dhivehi'. Of the remaining islands about a 100 have been developed into exotic resort islands that offer tourists their own hideaway. The islands of Maldives are very low lying with the highest point at approximately 8 feet above sea level. So, the Maldives government is trying to alleviate the worst effects of climate change to avoid sea levels rising, which may mean that within 100 years the Maldives could become uninhabitable. All new resorts are subject to a rigorous environmental impact study and developers are allowed to build on only 20% of the islands.

Accommodation certainly doesn't come cheap in the Maldives, but for that once-in-a-lifetime experience, it is definitely justified. The two options are staying on an island resort or a liveaboard (or both if you have the time). Many travellers also 'island hop' and spend a week or two on different islands, which can offer a variety of experiences, while some prefer the liveaboard option, which can offer incredible opportunities for surfing or scuba diving.

The Maldives is the destination for anyone looking for a uniquely indulgent break, breathtaking nature and sheer beauty, and memories that will stay with the family for a lifetime.

🛏 Fun Facts

Capital: Malé.

Population: 350,000.

Currency: Maldivian Rufiyaa.

Languages: Dhivehi (official), English (widely spoken).

Trivia: The Maldives were the first country in the world to hold an official presidential cabinet meeting underwater. During the meeting, which the president and vice president attended, a declaration on global climate change was signed.

Getting there and exploring around

The main airlines flying in from Europe are the UK, German & Italian charter flights which fly direct. Main scheduled services from Europe are those airlines flying direct: Sri Lankan Airways out of Heathrow and British Airways out of Gatwick and those flying via their main hub: Qatar Airways via Doha, Emirates via Dubai and Oman Airways via Muscat, and recently Ethad have started flying out of Abu Dhabi. Sri Lankan also have flights via Colombo.

After landing on the narrow strip of the Malé international airport, you need to catch either a boat or seaplane to your actual destination. If you are going to a tourist resort, hotel, or safari cruise, hotel staff will most likely pick you up upon arrival to guide you to the hotel's own transfer. You have the option of using a speedboat, seaplane, or local dhoni where offered.

Seaplanes are often used as a quicker option by tourist resorts located atolls further from the airport. Catching a seaplane is a rare treat that adds an extra layer to your experience of the Maldives by putting its unique geography into perspective. Travelling by speedboat too, is, on its own a fun adventure. Dhoni, the local boat used for travelling by locals is a gentler, but by no means a less enjoyable means of getting there. If you have very young children it may make sense to fly by sea-plane to save on time.

Best time of year to visit

The Maldives has a tropical climate distinguished by two seasons: the dry northeast monsoon which runs from December to March, and the wet southwestern monsoon from May to November, with more strong winds and rain. April is a transitional period noted for clear water and heat. The temperature remains remarkably consistent all year at around 30°C.

The Maldives specialises in winter sun for Europeans, making high season December to April, when the islands enjoy the dry monsoon. February to April is the hottest period and resorts are almost all operating at capacity during this period. Mid-December to early January comes at even more of a premium due to Christmas and New Year and prices are even higher. Easter and the Italian holiday week in August also attract peak prices at most resorts, especially the Italian-oriented ones.

From May to November is the period when storms and rain are more likely. It's still warm, but skies can be cloudy and the humidity is higher. This is the low season, with fewer people and lower prices. Diving is good year-round, although a basic rule is that life on the reef is more varied and visibility better on the western side of any atoll from May to November and from the eastern side of any atoll December to April. This means you'd be wise to choose your resort accordingly.

FUN FAMILY FACT:
Boduberu may not be the only form of music and dance in the Maldives but it is by far the most popular. Boduberu troupes consisting of 3-4 drummers, a lead singer and dancers perform at most resorts and in local villages on special holidays.

? Must know before you go

Mosquitoes. As the Maldives is tropical, there is no getting away from the blood sucking insects. They can be particularly rife during the rainy season, and it's wise to take caution especially with young children and babies. Stay inside during dawn and dusk, and use a net over the cot/bed at night. During the day you can find many safe insect repellent products to use on their skin, including 'stick-on' patches for prams & pushchairs.

Sunshine bewares. Overexposure to the sun is the most common aliment afflicting tourists to the Maldives. Apply sunscreen to all exposed areas, including your child's nose, ears, and toes, before you set out for the beach and repeat applications throughout the day. Limit the number of hours they play under the sun, especially in the first few days.

Traditions. Islam is the predominant religion in the Maldives. However, the resort islands are very relaxed and casual dress is the norm. Note though that beachwear is not acceptable in the restaurant(s) on resort islands or away from the resorts. Guests entering the restaurant in swimwear will be asked by a member of staff to cover up.

Highlights

North Malé Atoll. Enjoying indulgence and luxury at one of the finest island resorts in the world.

Haa Alif Atoll. Getaway up north in the chic hideaway of the Beach House.

South Malé Atoll. Dive in style at the Anantara Dhigu.

Markets in Malé. Observing local life and buying fresh fruit and vegetables at the local market.

👍 Tip for the Trip

"Can't face long-haul with a baby or toddler? Flying with toddlers can be challenging as they get bored easily, and it can be stressful with small babies if they are unsettled and cry. It makes sense to stop-over en-route, wherever possible. Breaking up the journey may take longer to reach your destination, but it is sometimes cheaper to travel indirectly and will offer the family a chance to see somewhere different and stretch legs!"

Adventure:
Food + Discovery
Destination: North Malé Atoll

Regional Information

The North Malé atoll is exactly that – north of Malé. It is also the main hub of tourism within the Maldives and boasts the largest number of resorts. Sometimes known as Maléatholhu Uthutuburi, it is of irregular shape, 58 kilometres long and contains about 50 islands (including the capital Malé). There are also sandbanks, coral patches, innumerable farus and submerged shoals (called 'haa' in Dhivehi). The general depths of the interior are between 25 and 35 fathoms (46 to 64 metres). Seen from space it is considered one of the most beautiful atolls on the planet. As it is fairly close to Malé airport, transfers here are normally by speed boat and take up to 1 hour to reach.

Maldivian Islands may disappear when the currents on the reef change. Maldivians call this strange phenomenon of erosion 'giramun dhiyun'. New islands also may appear, beginning as sandbanks or coral gravel heaps at another location of the reef (a phenomenon that is known among Maldivians as 'vodemun dhiyun'). Therefore, in the Maldives, islands are constantly eroding and constantly being formed. Human action, in the form of jetties or the dredging of channels on the reef, may change the pattern of currents on the reef and accelerate erosion. Partly why the Maldivian Government are keen to invoke a 'green' ethos to avoid further erosion of the islands.

The atolls in Maldives are often separated from each other by vast expanses of the deepest ocean; but despite the great distances, the daily life of Maldivians in the individual inhabited islands shows very few differences all along the length of the atoll chain.

Like all the islands in the North Malé Atoll, it is popular with scuba divers and snorkelers, and these are also legendary for those who have never dived before – it is a perfect opportunity to learn in warm waters and with sunshine, and plenty of the resorts have their own fully-equipped diving schools.

These island resorts are worlds in themselves; some of the larger ones offer different restaurants featuring local and continental cuisine along with exotic buffets.

Adventure: Food + Discovery
Destination: North Malé Atoll

Because fish and coconuts are the only items that don't have to be imported, they find their way onto most menus and spinybacked lobster is a particular delicacy. Needless to say the majority of the more taxing activities are sea based, with most resorts offering windsurfing, catamaran sailing, canoeing and water-skiing. You'll find the nearest thing to sightseeing is a leisurely trip in a local boat known as a dhoni, in search of an ideal picnic or beach spot.

Another feature of the North Malé Atoll is surfing. Surfing in Maldives has been increasingly gaining popularity. There are various surf travel operators who organise the surfing safaris to the outer atolls. If you go about pursuing a surfing sport in Maldives, you will have an ultimate experience of visiting the tropical island paradise. The ideal time for surfing is from March to November, when the wind conditions are perfect. Some of the best surf points are 'Chickens' - which is a popular surf point in Villingilimathi Huraa (Kuda Villingili), an uninhabited island. It lies on the eastern reef of North Malé. Cokes is another well-known surf point that is worth a visit too and Gurus is another popular surf point in Eastern reef of Malé. It is sited on Southern tip of North Malé Atoll.

Popular with the younger crowd is Honky, yet another surf point in Malé in Maldives. Situated in Thamburudhoo, which is an uninhabited island, it lies on the Eastern Reef of North Malé Atoll.

As the most populous atoll there are many resorts to chose from. For most of the part there are plenty of the five-star options such as One & Only Reethi Rah, Huvafen Fushi and the Four Seasons. However, there are also some good value-for-money resorts, which offer the same 'Maldivian experience' at a fraction of the price, such as Bandos.

Many of the island resorts also offer excellent Maldivian dining experiences. Most popular is a beach style Maldivian barbecue, often cooked on-site by a chef and served by a private butler. It is obviously popular with honeymoon couples who want to relax in the privacy of their bungalow, but equally enjoyable for families too, especially as children can pick their fish dish and enjoy watching it being cook it on the BBQ, while eating it camped out on the beach. It is an amazing special dining experience, and children certainly won't be bored while waiting for their food to arrive.

One & Only Reethi Rah

Pure indulgent, polished and plush –as far as island resorts go they don't come any better than this. Each unique villa has separate bathrooms, bedrooms, outside dining areas, and some have private pools. On arrival, (after a luxury yacht transfer) you are assigned your own private butler, which will become your friend and confident, tending to all your needs. The 'KidsOnly' playhouse is pretty special too. It is not the kind of resort that you will see hoards of children, but if needed, they are well looked after by a team of kind, and experienced staff. The signature KidsOnly programme provides children ages four to 11 and teens ages 12 to 17 with an exciting roster of activities and facilities, such as treasure hunts and baking.

For babies and toddlers, the resort offers professional baby-sitting services at a nominal fee, as well as items such as bottle warmers, sterilisers and baby monitor sets. Complimentary cots for children below the age of three are available upon request. Babies even get their own amenity kit on arrival.

There are also several dining options, but by far the most popular with families is the main 'Reethi restaurant' which has floor to glass windows and an 'open-view' kitchen, often used as a 'buffet-style'. For young weaners, they even have homemade purees, and fresh vegetable options. Probably by far the most important aspect of this property is that it doesn't feel overwhelming or crowded and you can easily find a corner of paradise to relax in peace with your family.

Guide Price: From £900 per villa per night
Best Room: Duplex Beach Villa

Adventure:
Action + Adventure
Destination: Haa Alif Atoll

Junior 7-11

Teen 12-16

✈ **Regional Information**

The Haa Alif Atoll - officially referred as 'Thiladhunmathi Uthuruburi' (Northern Thiladhunmathi Atoll) is situated in the northernmost administrative division of the Maldives. It is third largest atoll in the Maldives in terms of population and land area, and is the closest to Sri Lanka and India. As it is the furthest away from Malé, it can be a mission to reach, and usually a domestic flight to Hanimaadhoo (around 50 minutes) and then a speed boat transfer to reach your resort is the main method, which after a long flight is not always easy with young children. An expensive and quicker way is the seaplane option. In total Haa Alif Atoll contains 42 islands, 14 of which are inhabited. At present there are three tourist resorts in the atoll, Island Hideaway, Cinnamon Island Alidhoo and The Beach House all which offer varying experiences on different budgets.

Hanimaadhoo, where the local airport is based, is one of the inhabited islands and home to the Hanimaadhoo Meteorological Observatory. Many flight scientific research such as those investigating aerosol concentrations in the atmosphere and the Brown Cloud phenomenon have been initiated from Hanimaadhoo. Islanders from Hathifushi and Hondaidhoo have been relocated to Hanimaadhoo in the recent years, and it is planned to be one of the developmental centres of the newly planned Mathi-Uthuru Province. Although there are guesthouse options on Hanimaadhoo, most travellers don't stay here but stop for a hour to wait for onwards flights. The Maldives is renowned around the world as one of the top dive destinations. The country is home to over a thousand beautiful reefs boasting an abundant and diverse range of marine life. Almost all the resorts have PADI certified dive centres housing, and in this atoll it is no exception. Probably one of the major features is that this area, while it offers diving for both beginners and advanced, it isn't heavily populated, so many dive sites are pristine and the reefs are well maintained. There is also a stunning and wide range of sea-life here including dolphins, sharks, manta rays, napoleon fish and turtles. The Manta rays (which will mesmerise children) are very common in the season from December until

May and with 'cleaning stations', give divers the opportunity to enjoy their movements at a shallow depth very close by. PADI have several courses of introductory diving for children. Starting with 'Bubblemaker' (for aged 8+), which is a good way to start diving in a pool environment, the progressing onto 'Seal Team' (aged 8+) for young divers who are looking for action-packed fun in a pool by doing exciting scuba AquaMissions. Divers are introduced to underwater photography, navigation, environmental awareness and more. From aged 10-14 children can take part in the full PADI Open Water Diver programme and upon completion will become Junior Open Water Divers with certain age limitations for scuba diving. By learning to dive children gain so much understanding about the ocean, a sense of achievement from qualifying and will really enjoy sharing this past-time with their parents.

Other action and adventure activities in this atoll include deep sea fishing and windsurfing, which when there are strong winds, especially in the monsoon, create ideal conditions.

The waters around the Maldives offer some of the world's best deep-sea fishing grounds. Whether on a traditional 'dhoni' or fully equipped fishing boat, this sport is an exhilarating experience. The best time for fishing is usually during the monsoon seasons: the Hulhangu from May to September and Iruvai from December to April. Day excursions fishing can be arranged via most resorts.

A trip to the Haa Alif Atoll is an ideal experience for older children who will particularly love the vast range of watersports on offer, and also parents who want to escape the more crowded island atolls. As it can be tricky to reach, at least a week or two should be spent here to make the most of it.

Place to Stay and Eat

Beach House, Waldorf Astoria

Beach House Maldives, which is part of The Waldorf Astoria Collection, is located on the pristine, lagoon-ringed Haa Alif Atoll which is fringed by powder-white beaches and complemented with an unspoilt jungle-filled interior. The 35-acre resort comprises 83 Maldivian-style villas, three restaurants, four bars and a super luxurious spa. For children of all ages this is a paradise, but older children will particularly enjoy the dive centre which offers free snorkeling gear and for rainy days there is a 'sound proof' karaoke booth. Extensive sports activities including tennis, badminton and beach volleyball and complementary non-motorised water-sports such as wind-surfing, catamaran sailing and canoeing can also be enjoyed as a family pursuit. Adrenalin junkies shouldn't miss the bungee trampoline, which is a highlight for children and parents alike. The resort also offers a variety of authentic experiences such as visits to neighbouring islands and Maldivian afternoon tea experiences.

Guide Price: From £430 per villa per night
Best Room: Grand Beach Pavilion. A private, luxurious 600m² retreat featuring two bedrooms and two open-air bathrooms

Opposite page. Top. The Coral Project at The Beach House. **Bottom.** The Amazon Pool at The Beach House. **This page. Top.** Ocean Villa at The Beach House. **Bottom.** Surf & Turf at The Beach House.

Adventure:
Education + Hands On
Destination: South Malé Atoll

IDEAL FOR
**ALL
AGES**

+ Regional Information

Maléatholhu Dhekunuburi also known as South Malé Atoll is separated from North Malé Atoll by a deep channel (Vaadhu Kandu). Oblong in shape, this atoll is 35 kilometre in length. It contains 22 islands; all except for 5 are situated in its eastern fringes. Inside this atoll there are also many reefs and little coral patches which make navigation by boat sometimes difficult, but nevertheless it's not too far from Malé airport which makes this atoll accessible even for very young children.

All over Maldives, the origin of the culture of Maldives is shrouded with mystery. Although it is thought to have derived from a number of sources, the most important of which are its proximity to the shores of Sri Lanka and South India. Since the 12th century A.D. there are also influences from Arabia in the language and culture of the Maldives because of the general conversion to Islam in the 12th century, and its location as a crossroads in the central Indian Ocean. These cultural influences are witnessed in its language, cuisine, traditions and festivals.

Although, several languages are spoken in Maldives, the most common one is Divehi, meaning 'island'. Its roots are in Sanskrit and it is very similar to languages from Sri Lanka, South East Asia and North India containing several Arabic, Hindi and English words. Dhivehi is a fascinating language and it is always met with much enthusiasm when travellers learn a few words of Dhivehi.

Visiting the Maldives will also give you the chance to sample traditional Maldivian cuisine, and also try your hand at cooking. Being a chain of islands, the seafood is really the specialty in Maldives, and are prepared using local ingredients and spices. Garudhiya or the Tuna Soup, Spicy Curry and Rice are the staple diet of most of the people. The commonly eaten fish are Trevallies, Barracuda and Tuna served with various curries. The food here can taste from spicy and hot to mild and sweet. And like the language and culture, the cuisine of Maldives is influenced by the cooking style of

India and Sri Lanka but with distinct flavour of its own. Many western dishes like pasta are now part of the local cuisine but it is modified to give a regional taste. Chicken and other meats are normally prepared on celebrations and special occasions. The tropical fruits and dessert complete the list of a typical Maldives menu. Maldivian food is relatively easy to prepare, and even children who take an interest in cooking will enjoy spending a few hours in the kitchen cooking up a feast.

The festivals in Maldives bring with it a galore of colourful and exciting celebrations. Considering the number of special events the Maldivians celebrate, they can be divided into a broader category of religious and national festivals.

Religious festivals are celebrated in accordance with the lunar calendar, so the calendar date and the actual festival date may vary often. Whereas national festivals are always celebrated on significant fixed dates.

Maldivians are always game for an excuse to celebrate; there is much excitement and keenness along with the painstaking preparations. The people of Maldives follow all the festivals and events of the Islamic calendar, most popular being Ramadan, Bodu Eid (Eid-ul Al'haa) and Kuda Eid, (Eid-ul Fitr). If you happen to be travelling at the time of a major festival, it will be a magnificent experience for the whole family.

Anantara Dhigu

Dhigufinolhu Island is home to the Anantara Dhigu Resort & Spa, comprising of 110 spacious luxury villas, some with private plunge pools and just a 35 minute speedboat ride from Malé International Airport, so it is suitable for even very young children. They have an on-site cookery school, and children will enjoy being a chef for the day with aprons and hats - recreating traditional Maldivian, Thai and fusion dishes. They also have a programme of morning meditation and yoga for parents, and a spa offering traditional Maldivian treatments.

They have an on-site Kids Club, a pirate designed Dhoni club house with an abundance of enriching activities for guests of 11 and under to explore. A Kids Complete option on the kids menu offers a balanced meal to take care of daily dietary requirements, allowing parents to follow their home routine even while on holiday. Anantara Dhigu's family offering includes three complimentary meals a day for kids of 6 years and under when dining with their parents. Children aged 7 to 11 enjoy a 50 percent discount on all restaurant menus.

Best Room: A 2 bedroom Sunset Family Villa - one with a king size bed and the other with two single beds and room for a third single bed or baby cot

Guide Price: From £600 per villa per night

Opposite page. South Malé © Brian Knutsen. **This page, from top.** Aerial shot of Anantara Dhigu. Petal filled bath at Anantara Dhigu. Jetty at Anantara Dhigu.

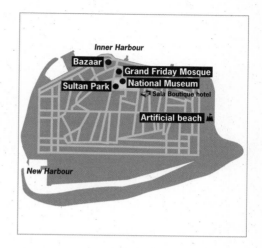

Focus On...
Malé

Malé is interesting to visit mainly for a taste of Maldivian life more than for its inherent wealth of things to see and do. Independent travellers will find that this is a great place to spend a day or two – it's also one of the few places where palm trees and sandy beaches aren't on the menu. The capital city is located on a separate island from the airport, so you will need to take a small ferry called a 'dhoni' across the capital which takes around 15 minutes.

Malé is pleasant and pleasingly quirky – its alcohol-free bars and restaurants jostle with its incredible array of shops and lively markets (imagine that in this tiny space all imports into the country are administered and sold) and the general hubbub of a capital is very much present. This is a chance to get a real feel for the Maldives, what makes its people tick and to meet Maldivians on an equal footing. There are several interesting places to visit, such as the 'Friday Mosque' an ancient mosque built in 1656 during the reign of Sultan Ibrahim Iskandar I, the interiors are intricately carved with Arabic writings and ornamental patterns. Unfortunately non-Muslims aren't allowed inside, but it's worth a visit anyway.

The local market, which is in the same area of the fish market, boats a range of indigenous fruits and vegetables which can make a tasty picnic for families on the hop. You can also find 'breadfruit chips' which are a traditional Maldivian snack and bottles of homemade pickles.

The National Museum located inside the Sultan Park houses a collection of traditional antiques, artefacts, royal regalia and old photographs, it's worth a look for a couple of hours. The Sultan park itself is one of the few green spaces in Malé, and is popular amongst tour guides as a place to take tourists, and a common destination on Friday evenings for young children and their parents.

For cooling down, Malé also has an 'artificial beach', it was built for locals as Malé lost its natural beaches (due to land reclamation). It's a popular hang-out for locals, families and children, and there is a 'lagoon' area which boasts a volleyball court and basketball court. Malé is home to a number of hotels, guest houses and inns. The 'Sala Boutique hotel' is a small, family owned property located near to the 'Peoples' Majilis'. With just 6 themed 'Thai' inspired rooms, all with organic amenities and private bathrooms from £100 per room per night, this place offers families excellent value for money, while staying in a central location. They also offer a traditional Thai 'foot rub' service and reflexology.

ⓘ Stylish Essentials

General Information

Maldives Tourist Information
www.visitmaldives.com

Maldives Transport and Contracting Company
www.mtcc.com.mv
T. +960 (0) 332 6822
E. info@mtcc.com.mv

Maldivian Air Taxi
Malé International Airport
Malé
www.maldivianairtaxi.com
T. +960 (0) 331 5203
E. info@maldivianairtaxi.com

Trans Maldivian Airways
PO Box 2079
Malé International Airport
Republic of Maldives
www.tma.com.mv
T.+960 3348400

Emirates
www.emirates.com
T. +44 (0) 844 800 2777 9
(UK call centre)

Etihad
www.etihadairways.com
T. +44 (0) 203 450 7300 (UK
reservations & ticketing)

Malaysian Airlines
www.malaysiaairlines.com
T. +603 (0)7843 3000
(24 hour ticketing, lost baggage etc)

Qatar Airways
www.qatarairways.com
T. +44 (0) 870 389 8090
(UK Reservations)

Sri Lankan Airlines
www.srilankan.lk
T. +44 (0) 330 808 0800
(UK Reservations & Tickets)
E. reservations@srilankan.aero

PADI
Professional Association
of Diving Instructors
Information on diving courses
& centres worldwide
www.padi.com
T. +44 (0) 117 300 7234
(European reservations)

The official publication of The Liveaboard Association
Liveaboards of Maldives
4th Floor, Ma. Uthuruvehi, Keneri Magu
Malé
www.liveaboardassociation.mv
T. +960 (0) 3300 640
E. info@liveabordassociation.mv

Yacht Charter Information & Bookings
www.yachtcharterguide.com
T. +44 (0) 131 666 2555
E. info@yachting.org

North Malé Atoll

One & Only Reethi Rah
North Malé Atoll
Maldives
www.oneandonlyresorts.com
T. + 960 (0) 664 8800
(Reservations)
E. reservations@oneandonly
reethirah.com

South Malé Atoll

Anantara Dhigu
Dhigufinolhu South Malé Atoll 20109,
Maldives
www.anantara.com
T. +960 (0) 664 4100

Haa Alif Atoll

Beach House, Waldorf Astoria
www.beachhousemaldives.com
T. +960 (0) 650 0408
E. reservations@beachhouse
maldives.com

Malé

Old Friday Mosque
Malé
T. +960 (0) 3323224

National Museum & Sultan Park
Medhuziyaarai Magu
Malé
T. +960 (0) 3322254
Open Saturday to Thursday
9.00–15.00, closed public holidays.

Aïoli Restaurant
Lotus Goalhi
Malé
www.aioli.com.mv
T. +960 (0) 330 4984

Sala Boutique Hotel
Malé
www.salafamilymaldives.com
T. +960 (0) 334 5959
E. info@salafamilymaldives.com

Serengeti by night, Under Canvas © &Beyond.

TANZANIA

Serengeti National Park | Kilimanjaro & Arusha |
Zanzibar | Pemba Island

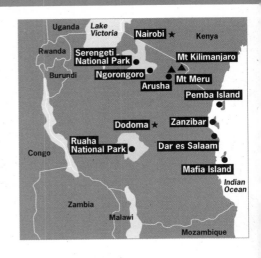

🏆 Why is this place so special?

Perched on the edge of the African continent, and facing the Indian Ocean, Tanzania is east Africa's largest country and over a quarter of its surface area its taken up in national parks and game reserves which, collectively, harbour over 20% of Africa's large mammal population. During the great migration, it is also home to over a million migrating wildebeest and zebra - one of the most scintillating wildlife spectacles on the planet and definitely a highlight for the ultimate safari trip.

Tanzania is without doubt one of the top safari destinations in Africa. Experience the vast expanse of flat savannah grasses of the Serengeti National Park, the spectacular wildlife at the Ngorongoro Crater or the dramatic Tanzanian section of the Rift Valley at Lake Manyara. Tanzania's numerous national safari parks offer game viewing that is second to none. The safari not only offers children the ultimate experience of getting up close and personal with wildlife but importantly spending quality time together as a family on game drives can be a great bonding experience. Socialising with other adults too, can really help improve their social skills.

Kilimanjaro, standing at 19,336ft, is Africa's highest mountain and offers a fantastic starting place for a safari, or if you are brave enough (and fit enough) spend 6 days climbing to the summit. There are many different routes to the summit if you want to conquer the snow-capped peak, and once climbed your adrenaline will be rushing for days on end. And, yes, it can be done with children.

For those who are just looking to relax with their families, Zanzibar and its surrounding islands off the east coast have stunning white sandy beaches and excellent coral reefs for diving excursions. The warm Indian Ocean makes Zanzibar a perfect relaxing getaway and a stunning change of scenery from Tanzania's game reserves and national parks, a great destination for a beach break or at the end of an action packed safari trip.

Accommodation options are vast and varied. It is possible to stay in some of Africa's most luxurious lodges, (with private pools and butlers) or camp it out with the herds of elephant and giraffe, or simply rent a basic beach hut on the coast for next to nothing. There is something for most budgets and tastes.

Tanzania is primarily perfect for older children and teenagers, due to the restrictions on game safaris, however safari camps are increasingly changing their policies to accommodate much younger children in an attempt to widen their market. If you have children of varying ages, then consider a low key safari experience and then some beach time on the coast, for a family adventure of a lifetime –no-one will be disappointed with Tanzania.

📖 Fun Facts

Capital: Dodoma.

Population: 44 million.

Currency: Tanzanian Shilling.

Languages: Kiswahili or Swahili (official), English (primary language of commerce), Arabic (widely spoken in Zanzibar) and many local languages.

Trivia: The Great Rift Valley, a 6,000-mile crack (fissure), which runs through the middle of Tanzania, was formed twenty million years ago; it was created when the earth's crust ripped apart.

⚓ Getting there and exploring around

Tanzania has two main international airports, one outside the commercial capital Dar es Salaam, and the other near Arusha (and Mount Kilimanjaro) called Kilimanjaro International Airport. Charter flights and some international operators do fly directly to Zanzibar Island.

If you're planning to visit Northern Tanzania, the best airport to arrive at is Kilimanjaro International Airport. KLM has daily flights from Amsterdam. Ethiopian and Kenya Airways also fly into KIA. If you are planning to visit Zanzibar, you'll want to fly to the capital Dar es Salaam. European carriers that fly into Dar es Salaam include British Airways, KLM and Swissair.

There are numerous ways and means of getting around Tanzania, depending on how much time you have. Flying around is the usual option and Precision Air offers routes between all the major Tanzanian towns. Regional Air Services offers flights to Grumeti (Serengeti), Manyara, Sasakwa, Seronera, Dar es Salaam, Arusha and more. For quick flights to Zanzibar from around Tanzania, check out ZanAir.

Local ferries also pass between Zanzibar and Pemba Islands and there are several daily high-speed ferries from the port in Dar es Salaam to Stone Town on Zanzibar. The trip takes about an hour and a half and tickets can be bought on the spot from the ticket office for US Dollars. Note: A very slow boat can take up to 14 hours to make the journey.

A popular way to get around big towns and cities, or for shorter distances, is with a dalla-dalla (mini-bus). Dalla-dallas are privately owned and usually crammed with way too many people, and they travel along set routes but you can disembark wherever you want for the most part (if you can squeeze yourself out). Dalla-dallas are very cheap and a fun way to get around.

☼ Best time of year to visit

Tanzania lies just south of the equator and on the whole enjoys a tropical climate. There are two rainy seasons, generally the heaviest rains (called Masika) usually fall from mid-March to May and a shorter period of rain (called Mvuli) from November to mid-January. The dry season, with cooler temperatures, lasts from May to October.

The best time to visit Tanzania is during the main dry season, from May to October. The rains make access to some of Tanzania's parks and reserves difficult, and trekking also becomes a little more cumbersome.

If you want to see the Great Annual Migration of millions of zebra and wildebeest unfold, then best time to witness the migration is probably February - March when the wildebeest and zebra have their young. Not only can you enjoy seeing baby animals, but the predators are at the highest number too. The migration usually moves out of the Serengeti area by the end of June and doesn't return until December. December through March can get quite hot and humid, especially in Western and Southern Tanzania which makes it a little uncomfortable to spend a lot of time in the bush, so this time isn't ideal with children.

As Mount Kilimanjaro and Mount Meru are a stones throw away from one another, so the trekking seasons are basically the same. The best time to trek is January - March and September - October.

? Must know before you go

Safari essentials. Whilst most lodges now are accepting children, the general rule of thumb is wait until the children are at least 10 years old before taking them on safari. They are then at an age to appreciate the experience. Safaris usually involve long periods in 4x4 vehicles, once the novelty has worn off, can be boring for kids!

Visas & vaccines. Most nationalities need a tourist visa to enter Tanzania; they are valid for 6 months from the date of issue. You can obtain a visa at all airports in Tanzania as well as at the border crossings, but it is advisable to get a visa beforehand, as queues and waiting times can be bad. Check directly with a Tanzanian Embassy for fees and procedures before departure. To visit Tanzania you generally require a Malaria & Yellow Fever inoculation, although check with a travel clinic.

Local know-how. Tanzanians are well known for their friendly, laid-back attitude. In most cases you will be humbled by their hospitality despite the fact that most people are a lot poorer than you. As you travel in the touristy areas, you will probably attract your fair share of souvenir hawkers and beggars. Remember that these are poor people who are trying to earn money to feed their families. If you aren't interested then say so, but try and remain polite. Try not to wear lots of jewellery, or walk around on empty beaches at night, which can attract petty crime.

Highlights

Serengeti in Style. Spending a few nights under canvas in a mobile tented camp or in a luxurious lodge.

Trek of a Lifetime. Africa's highest peak, Kilimanjaro, offers a breathtaking 7 day hike to its summit.

Discovering Zanzibar. Zanzibar is one of Tanzania's biggest tourist draws and a popular add-on after a dusty safari. You can enjoy spice tours near Stone Town, snorkelling, scuba diving.

Pemba. Take 'dhow' boat around the beautiful and sparsely inhabited island of Pemba

FUN FAMILY FACT:
Every country in the world has its superstitions, and Tanzania is no exception. Babies in Tanzania are often painted with eyeliner (kohl) around their eyes to ward off evil spirits or bad emotions. This is most common in Zanzibar & Pemba.

 Tip for the Trip

"Game drives can be long and sometimes boring for children, as spotting wildlife can be tricky. Buy them a camera, let them use binoculars and give them 'wildlife' check-list to mark off what they have seen. Finally, drives can get cooler (especially early mornings) so take plenty of layers of clothing."

Adventure: Nature + Wildlife
Destination:
Serengeti National Park

✦ Regional Information

Serengeti National Park is one of the best-known wildlife sanctuaries in the world, and symbolises the classic African safari. With more than 2 million wildebeest, half a million Thomson's gazelle, and a quarter of a million zebra, it has the greatest concentration of plains game in Africa. The Serengeti is also synonymous with the annual wildebeest and zebra migration.

The annual migration is a truly remarkable wildlife show and worth planning for. The best time to witness the migration is February to March when the wildebeest and zebra have their young. Not only can you enjoy seeing baby animals, but the predators are at the highest number too. Because the herds also concentrate in the south of the Serengeti, it's easy to plan your wildlife viewing in that area and find a safari company that offers lodging there – and lets face it - there are so many options to choose from low budget to luxury mobile tents. A safari experience as a family is really a once-in-a-lifetime trip, children will love being immersed in nature, spotting wildlife from a 4x4 jeep, going on 'bush walks', and some lodges also provide campfires and star gazing at night.

Wildlife viewing is best in the early morning and late afternoon, when temperatures are cooler and wildlife is easier to spot. While this means that the whole family has to be up and ready by 5 or 6 am, spotting animals is so exciting that even the sleepiest in the children are likely to accept the change to his or her biological clock and fall in step with the rhythm of the bush.

The name 'Serengeti' comes from the Maasai language and means an 'extended place'. The National Park alone covers an area of 12,950 square kilometres. The Serengeti ecosystem, which includes the following main reserves, Ngorongoro Conservation Area, the Grumeti Game Reserve, the Maswa Game Reserve, the Maasai Mara Game reserve (in Kenya) and numerous concession areas, is roughly the size of Sicily. It lies between the shores of Lake Victoria in the west, Lake Eyasi in the south, and the Great Rift Valley to the east.

Adventure: Nature + Wildlife
Destination: Serengeti National Park

The Serengeti is not fenced and is surrounded by a number of huge reserves and private concessions, so any given day of the year you can expect the unexpected in terms of wildlife watching. Together with the National Park these make the greater Serengeti ecosystem. The 'Serengeti' also forms part of what is commonly know as the 'Northern Circuit', and many chose to fly into Arusha, to start a planned 5 or 6 day minimum safari, which takes into all the main reserves, including the Ngorongoro crater Lake Manyara, and Tarangire. This is the most common safari circuit in Tanzania and often the least expensive option. Many safari goers these days are as interested in visiting local tribes as they are spotting the 'Big Five'. Most safaris will include a visit to a Maasai village, school or an organized hunt with the local Hadzabe.

The Ngorongoro Conservation area which borders the Serengeti in northern Tanzania and includes the world's largest crater which acts as a natural enclosure for almost every type of species found in East Africa. This includes the very rare black rhino. The Ngorongoro Crater is where you'll witness some of the densest population of wildlife in the world and it's a truly amazing place for budding photographers. The Maasai still live within the conservation area, and it's also home to Olduvai where some of man's earliest remains have been found. There are many ways to experience the Ngorongoro area, such as a 'Hot Air Balloon' ride which offers an incredible 'birds-eye' view of the region, and can be a welcome break from the continuous game drives. If you have a spare morning or afternoon, it is an incredible experience especially for adventurous children. There are also many activities such as taking a picnic on the 'crater floor' or watching the local Maasai warriors wearing dancing in traditional dress and carrying flaming torches - in which travellers are encouraged to participate!

Lake Manyara is a relatively small national park but it's incredibly diverse. Lake Manyara boasts plenty of elephants, tree-climbing lions (getting rarer), leopards, giraffes and more than 400 species of birds including flocks of pink flamingos. Most organised safari itineraries stop at Lake Manyara for a night en route to the Serengeti and Ngorongoro (or on the way back to Arusha).

Tarangire, like Lake Manyara, is often combined with a visit to the larger, better known Serengeti and Ngorongoro parks. But during the dry season, (June to October) the river beds just teem with animals and it is well worth a trip. Tarangire is also good place to enjoy a walking safari on the ground and an excellent place to view elephants. Although be prepared to swat flies here, at certain times of the year they can get annoying.

The Serengeti National Park and the nearby reserves offers families such an incredible and diverse safari experience, from getting up close and personal to elephants, to watching the herds of Zebras. Whilst a safari is rarely a cheap experience, children and their parents, will certainly not be disappointed.

 **Places to Stay and Eat**

Serengeti Under Canvas

Serengeti Under Canvas offers 2 luxury mobile camps which roam the Serengeti plains and beyond. Each camp has 8 Bedouin style tents all with elegant finishes of Persian rugs and chandeliers. The semi-permanent camps move between various locations, staying off the beaten track and following the herds of buffalo and wildebeest that migrate across the Serengeti. It is ultra comfortable with stylish safari tents, large beds, and en-suite bathrooms with flush loos and bucket showers. Due to the design of the camp and the nature of walking safaris only children over 12 years of age are accepted to stay here.

Guide Price: From £406 pppn
Best Room: All tents!

Klein`s Camp

With just ten thatched stone cottages, Klein's Camp provides an experience that is both personal and intimate. Whitewashed walls and rich wooden floors, combined with soft cream furnishings, create a calm and soothing refuge from the adventures of the day. Inspired by the breathtaking natural backdrop, relax on your private veranda with a pair of binoculars. There is a pool and deck tucked into the hillside and the Safari Shop stocks locally made Maasai crafts. Klein's Camp is not really suited to very small children and therefore only accepts children over the age of 6.

Guide Price: From £406 pppn
Best Room: All

Ngorongoro Crater Lodge

The Crater Lodge has 30 suites, divided between three adjacent camps: North and South Camps, comprising twelve suites each, and the more intimate Tree Camp, with six suites. Each camp has its own viewing deck, grand sitting room and dining room with their entrances dramatically illuminated at night by large fire bowls. The stone-built suites all include a private viewing deck, fireplace, spacious en suite bathroom - with free-standing, chandelier-lit bathtub - and is discreetly attended by a private butler. Their luxurious, colonial-style interiors are decorated with sumptuous fabrics, gilt-framed mirrors and carved Zanzibar wood panelling, and the floor-to-ceiling windows have spectacular views of the crater. Although there are no specific child care facilities, children over 5 years old are welcome.

Guide Price: From £493 pppn
Best Room: A suite in the North Camp

Adventure:
Action + Adventure
Destination:
Kilimanjaro + Arusha

✦ **Regional Information**

At 19,336 feet, snow-capped Mount Kilimanjaro in Tanzania is Africa's highest peak.
It is the world's tallest walkable mountain, and what a walk it is. Ascending through five
different ecological zones just to reach the summit.

Kilimanjaro is the world's highest free standing, snow-covered equatorial mountain.
Images of the towering snow-covered cone rising majestically from fertile green foothills
have become a powerful motif of Tanzania's extraordinary extremes. Few could deny
a very distinct sense of awe when the cloud clears to reveal a glimpse of the towering
peaks, shining bright in the equatorial sun.

Kilimanjaro also represents a powerful life force for the local Chagga people and
all those who have made their lives around this mountain, providing rich volcanic soils
for agriculture and an endless source of pure spring waters.

One of the most amazing aspects of the mountain in the present day is the
accessibility of its peak to climbers with no real mountain climbing equipment or previous
experience of scaling such heights. Kilimanjaro is the highest mountain that regular
tourists can climb, although it remains a considerable feat of human endurance! The
breathable oxygen at the top is less than half the amount than is common at sea level,
and climbers cover at least eighty kilometres on nothing but their own two feet over
the five days it takes to reach the top and return. There are several routes to climb
Kilimanjaro, among them, Marangu, Rongai, Lemosho, Shira, Umbwe and Machame.

The number of climbers has escalated to over a thousand a year during the last
century, quite a development since Hans Meyer made history as the first European to
scale the highest point of Kilimanjaro in 1889. The increasing numbers each year have
made it necessary for the National Park to insist that all climbs are pre-booked, and
passes are no longer issued at the last minute at the park gate.

Although it is possible to simply trek a route to the pinnacle of Kibo without
relying on professional climbing equipment, it remains a hard and serious endeavour

Adventure: Action + Adventure
Destination: Kilimanjaro + Arusha

that requires a level of physical fitness, stamina and a realistic awareness of the potentially damaging effects of high altitudes. Many tour operators request that clients consult a doctor before attempting to scale the mountain, and have a physical check-up for overall fitness. The minimum climbing age is 12 years, but anyone between the ages of 12 to 16 needs to take extra care and be monitored very closely as altitude sickness can creep up on undeveloped bodies and be much more severe than in adults. If achieved this is the ultimate hike of a lifetime, and something your children will remember for the rest of their lives.

You can only climb Kilimanjaro with an organised trek and along established routes, so you have to go with an operator. The operators vary from excellent to downright negligent, so be selective and do not go to the cheapest. Many trekking companies offer a guide and also butlers (to help carry equipment), and some are large and some exclusive groups. It is important to do your research, book in advance (during the high season is best for weather conditions); break in your hiking boots and build up some stamina, especially if you have your children with you. It is also advisable to make sure your hike is at least 6-7 days for maximum success. Any shorter and you will not be properly acclimatised. Routes vary in degree of difficulty, traffic and scenic beauty. The least difficult routes are Marangu and Rongai; the more difficult routes are Machame, Shira and Limosho. The longer routes may have more difficult hiking but you'll be more acclimatised and your chances of reaching the summit are therefore higher. The longer western routes also allow you to start your summit day at a more reasonable hour. Accommodation along the trek is basic, staying in huts and camps, but this adds to the unique experience of the trek.

Reaching the summit is the hardest part of the trek (but the most satisfying). The final ascent is usually timed so you can watch the sunrise over the crater and distant plains. Enjoy the view take a few photos and get back down before you get too affected by the high altitude. Afterwards, climbers often take a well earned rest in a spot of luxury in nearby Arusha.

Arusha town, as previously mentioned, is often the starting point for trekkers and safari goers. It is also the finishing point, before flying onto other parts of Tanzania, such as Zanzibar or Pemba islands. It is the northern Tanzania's safari capital and Arusha National Park (a 40 minute drive from Arusha) is a multi-faceted jewel, often overlooked by safari goers, despite offering the opportunity to explore a beguiling diversity of habitats within a few hours. There are many accommodation options in Arusha itself, the Arusha national park and also in the Kilimanjaro national park, from camp sites to rest houses and lodges and mountain huts.

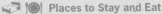 **Places to Stay and Eat**

Kilimanjaro Mountain Resort

Kilimanjaro Mountain Resort is located in the Kyalla village of Marangu. Set amongst shamba farms the lower slopes of Mount Kilimanjaro, this hotel is a primary base for treks. Although Kilimanjaro Mountain Resort is nothing to write home about, compared with other options in the area, it is generally pleasant, reasonably well equipped, clean and even has a small swimming pool. Children under 6 years are free.

Guide Price: From £110 prpn
Best Room: Go for the newly renovated twin room with a balcony with views of Kilimanjaro

Rivertrees

This lovely little lodge just outside Arusha, located in the foot hills of mount Meru and surrounded by streams, the tropical ambience creates a perfect night to either gather yourself before or after taking on Kili, and bodes well for the hard worked safari buff. The rooms and service are of great quality and the general feel is excellent value for money as well as great convenience. Each room and the main house at Rivertrees tells a different story stamped with its own character. They have an excellent chef who cooks great home-made food.

Guide Price: From £180 prpn
Best Room: Exclusive 'River House' with double accommodation for large families

Arusha Coffee Lodge

Located on the outskirts of Arusha town, and comprising of 30 Plantation Houses - including 12 Plantation Suites - Arusha Coffee Lodge has been designed around the original landowner's home which dates back over one hundred years. Within the main Plantation House resides a restaurant, an intimate bar and a cosy lounge, all of which possess inviting open log fires. Also has two boutiques, an enclosed and intimate swimming pool and a popular garden terrace, children under 3 are free. A great place to relax at the end of a trek or safari.

Guide Price: From £210 prpn (low season)
Best Room: A plantation suite with private deck patio

Adventure:
Education + Hands On
Destination: Zanzibar

Regional Information

Zanzibar is a fabulous (and easy) family destination where parents won't have to sacrifice quality for convenience. The Spice Islands (comprised of two main Islands, Unguja (also called Zanzibar Island), and Pemba, along with many smaller islands and atolls) has a friendly atmosphere, safe beaches, and beautiful seas, which make it a great spot for rest, relaxation, diving and learning about the unique history and culture in Stone Town (an old Arab town). It is a popular for families (even with young children) as a 2 week holiday in itself, but also as an add-on post-safari for 5 or 7 days. It is also very possible to arrange a trip to Zanzibar independently (without the need of a tour operator) meaning you will have much more flexibility, and if you are travelling in the quieter season, you don't necessarily have to book accommodation ahead of travelling, and just turn up to one of the many beach huts. Like the rest of Tanzania, it is also worth mentioning that it is only +3 hours ahead of GMT, so, despite a long flight, even young children can adapt to a new routine quickly.

   Zanzibar's history has undoubtedly been shaped by its geographical location. It is situated on the eastern edge of Africa within range of monsoon winds and ocean currents. For many years Zanzibar was a popular respite for ships travelling to Arabia, India and the Far East. Often sailors were obliged to spend many months resting and relaxing whilst they waited for the monsoon winds to change direction and gather strength for their journey home.

   It is thought that the first people to settle on Zanzibar were African fishermen who travelled across from Tanzania mainland around five to six thousand years ago. Since then Zanzibar's history has been forged by many external factors, evidence exists in the architecture and even the language, Kiswahili; which is a mixture of Arabic, Portuguese, English and Hindi words.

   Stone Town is located along the west coast of Zanzibar Island and is considered to be one of the most traditional of remaining old Swahili trading settlements that would

Adventure: Education + Hands On
Destination: Zanzibar

have been prevalent along East Africa. It resembles the labyrinth style medina's of north Africa and Morocco with all the narrow streets, twists and turns. It is definitely worth spending a night here to explore the town's history and nearby spice markets, before heading up to coast to the beach.

Zanzibar has some of the best beaches anywhere in Africa and arguably the world, the best of which are to be found along the east coast on the northern part of the island. The beaches in this region are protected by off shore coral reefs and have fine white coral sand. It is popular with backpackers, students, divers, families and honeymoon couples, so visitor wise it is varied. The best beaches lie at Matemwe for powdery white sand, Pongwe and Kendwa for easy swimming. Nungwi (located on the northernmost tip) is lively fusion of traditional and modern styles and is a destination in itself. The beach again boasts beautiful white sands and idyllic setting, whilst only a few steps back you will find a host of guesthouses, bars and restaurants. Nungwi definitely has the party atmosphere and is considered by some as the only place to be, however others (especially families) may choose to give it a wide berth in favour of more tranquil parts of the Island.

Learning to dive in Zanzibar is a dream. Zanzibar is reputed to have some of the best diving in the world, and the coral reef structures that surround Unguja and Pemba ensure that the marine life is abundant. Good visibility (20 - 60m) and a year-round average water temperature of 27°C ensure that you enjoy your Zanzibar diving experience, and also present an ideal opportunity for learning to dive or upgrading your diving qualification. There are several dive centres on the island, who offer beginner and more advanced courses.

If you want to add in a little safari experience to this beach trip then a short hop across from Dar Es Salaam is the 'Saadani National Park.' Where children can spot zebras, giraffe, and if you take a boat along the river you'll see hippos and crocodiles. It is a much slower pace than the other safari excursions, so it is ideal with children from age 6 upwards (and even younger). Spending a day or two here won't be the ultimate safari – but it will surely give you a taster, if you can't manage a full safari in the other national parks.

 Places to Stay

Serena Inn Stone Town
The hotel comprises two historic seafront buildings which house the 52 individually styled air-conditioned rooms and suites. Rooms have a strong Arabian influence and have balconies with stunning views of the sea. Stone Town itself has a strong Arabic influence which adds to the town's exoticism and it is well worth spending a day wandering its narrow, winding side streets during a stay on Zanzibar.

Guide Price: From £200 prpn
Best Room: Prime room

Essque Zalu Zanzibar
Located on the north east coast of Zanzibar, in a natural cove lies the luxurious Essque Zalu Zanzibar which is made up of suites and three to four bedroom villas. The hotel has its own Petit VIP club for children aged between four and twelve years old, keeping them busy with activities such as treasure hunts, cooking lessons, perfume making and cultural adventures.

Guide Price: From £310 prpn
Best Room: 3 bed ocean view villa

Baraza
Located on the east coast of Zanzibar, Baraza is a luxurious, family-friendly hotel with a variety of one and two bedroom villas set on a beautiful stretch of beach. Each of the villas comprises a living area with day-bed, large bathroom, private terrace and plunge pool. The two-bedroom villas are perfect for a family of four and there is also a children's club, large outdoor swimming pool, large spa with lap pool, yoga room, a gym and two tennis courts.

Guide Price: From £423 prpn
Best Room: Presidential Villa, with two bedrooms, a private garden and plunge pool

Places to Eat

Silk Route Restaurant, Stone Town
With its bright tapestries, hanging lights, and the delicious tandoori dishes and spicy curries this place is certainly is a little find. You might need some help to navigate the massive menu; let the staff steer you toward dishes like lamb in a creamy cashew sauce or jumbo shrimp in a rich butter sauce accented by ginger, garlic, coconut, and raisins. The Silk Route is also among the best in Stone Town for vegetarians, with dishes such as vegetable korma dressed in saffron, raisins, and nuts. Be sure to wash it down with a refreshing mango lassi.

Mercury's, Stone Town
With a lively beachfront setting and some of the best sunset views around, Mercury's is as much a Stone Town icon as the Old Fort itself. Named for Queen front man Freddie Mercury, who was born just down the road, this busy hangout serves up an eclectic menu with everything from fajitas and fish tacos to pastas and curries. Red snapper in green curry and grilled tuna with pesto mayo stand out among a host of good, if not unforgettable, fish dishes; more reliable are the delicious thin-crust pizzas. Live weekend music—from Congolese drummers to traditional taarab groups—packs in the tourist crowds.

Tower Top, Stone Town
The rooftop restaurant of the 236 Hurumzi Hotel, it boasts a sultan's-eye view of the Indian Ocean and the town's minarets and spires. Guests shed their shoes at the entrance and loll on bright pillows at low tables set on Persian carpets. The menu changes daily, with dishes featuring local vegetables, seafood, and spice-scented rice (expect to see dishes like fish in spice and onion sauce, served with raisin-studded rice and spinach with coconut milk).

Focus On...
Pemba Island

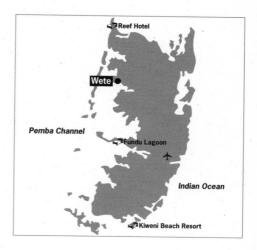

Pemba Island is the northernmost Island of the archipelago, and is considered to be part of Zanzibar. Pemba Island is still the world's major clove producer, but has now slipped into its more traditional role of being an Island. Transportation to and from Pemba Island is gradually improving these days. There are daily flights, ferries and Dhows from Mombasa, Dar Es Salaam, Zanzibar, Selous and Arusha.

Pemba was seized by the Sultan of Muscat (now Oman) in the 17th century. He was so enchanted by the Spice Islands that he installed himself in Zanzibar and ruled Muscat from there. When the Western Colonial powers came to East Africa the British forced the Sultanates of Muscat and Zanzibar to separate and then administered the Spice Islands in the name of the Sultan. All the while, the Arab dhows would ply the trade winds down from the Arabian Peninsula to East Africa. With the winds they would take cloves to India, textiles back to the Arab lands and silver and wood to the Spice Islands of Unguja and Pemba. The Dhows have remained a constant throughout the history of Pemba. To this day they still ply the run from Wete to Shimoni in Kenya and, when the winds are favourable they plough through to Northern Mozambique. Pemba is a magical island. Unlike Unguja, Pemba is hilly. Gentle, undulating hills and deep verdant valleys are all covered with a dense cover of clove, coconut and mango plantations.

Travelling in Pemba is like travelling in unknown territory. Visitors simply have to be prepared to 'rough it', unless staying at one of only a few decent accommodations. The only guesthouses on Pemba are at Mkoani, Chake Chake and Wete. All are very small, modest and with basic facilities. Food must be bought at the local markets and shops. Generally one of the only places to eat out is at the local stalls, or one of the few guesthouses. Transport is limited to a few taxis, private cars and the public bus service. Beyond this, walking is the only option, unless you have arranged pre-booked transfers

The luxury option is spending a few nights at 'Fundu Lagoon' which there are 18 spacious thatched and tented rooms, including 6 suites with private plunge pools, set on a raised wooden deck with wonderful ocean views. At high tide, the white sand beach is perfect for swimming, while at low tide the reef is exposed and one can explore miles of unspoilt seashore, with its unique marine and bird life. Nearby lies Misali Island, an idyllic sand atoll surrounded by some of Africa's best diving and snorkelling. There are no specific child care facilities here and the resort has a minimum age of 12 years, so perfect for older families.

General Information

Tanzania's Tourist Board
www.tanzaniatouristboard.com
T. + 255 (0) 22 2111244
E. safari@ud.co.tz

Official Information on National Parks
www.tanzaniaparks.com

Tanzania Travel Guides
www.tanzaniatourguide.com

Tanzania Embassy
Tanzania High Commission UK
3 Stratford Place W1C 1AS
London, UK
www.tanzaniahighcommission.co.uk
T. +44 (0) 207 569 1470
E. balozi@tanzania-online.gov.uk

Airlines

KLM
www.klm.com
T. +44 (0) 871 231 0000
(UK reservations)

Ethiopian Airlines
www.flyethiopian.com
T. +44 (0) 800 6350644
(UK reservations)

Kenya Airways
www.kenya-airways.com
T. +254 (0)20 642 2465
(ticket office)

SWISS International Airlines
www.swiss.com
T. +44 (0) 845 601 0956
(UK service centre)

British Airways
www.ba.com
T.+44 (0) 844 493 0787
(UK reservations)

Precision Air
NIC HDQ Building
Samora Av/Pamba Rd
PO Box 70770
Dar es Salaam, Tanzania
East Africa.
www.precisionairtz.com
T. +255 (0) 22 2130800
E. info@precisionairtz.com

Air Excel
www.airexcelonline.com
T. +255 (0) 27 254 8429
E. reservations@airexcelonline.com

Zanair
www.zanair.com
T.+255 (0) 24 2233670
E. reservations@zanair.com

Flightlink
www.flightlink.co.tz
T. +255 (0)782 354448
E. Dar-reservations@flightlink.co.tz

General Tour Operators

Tanzania Association of Tour Operators
www.tatotz.org
T. +255 (0) 27 250 4188
E. info@tatotz.org

The Tanzania Travel Company
www.tanzaniatravelcompany.com
T. +255 (0) 27 254 57 49
E. info@tanzaniatravelcompany.com

Elewana
Elewana Africa
Sopa Plaza
3rd Floor, 99 Serengeti Road
PO Box 12814 Arusha
www.elewanacollection.com
T. +255 (0) 27 250 0630
E. videar@elewana.com

Tanzania Odyssey
www.tanzaniaodyssey.com
T. +44 (0) 2074718780 (UK)
T. +1 (0) 866 356 4691
E. info@tanzaniaodyssey.com

Nomad Tanzania
www.nomad-tanzania.com
E. info@nomad-tanzania.com

Serengeti National Park

Serengeti Tourist Information
www.serengeti.org

Information on the Migration
www.wildwatch.com/great_migration

Ngorongoro Crater Conservation Authority
www.ngorongorocrater.org

Serengeti Under Canvas
www.serengetiundercanvas.com
T.+27 (0)11 809 4314

Klein's Camp
www.kleinscamp.com
T. +27 11 809 4314

Ngorongoro Crater Lodge
www.ngorongorocrater.com
T. +27 11 809 4314

Kilimanjaro & Arusha

Kilimanjaro Travel Guide
www.mtkilimanjarologue.com

Peak Planet
www.peakplanet.com

Kilimanjaro Climbing Companies
Team Kilimanjaro
www.teamkilimanjaro.com
T. +44 (0) 20 193 5895
E. info@teamkilimanjaro.com

Thomson Treks
Thomson Safaris, Ltd.
Box 6074
Arusha,
www.thomsontreks.com
T. +617 (0) 923 0426
E. info@thomsontreks.com

Serengeti Pride Safaris
Serengeti Pride Company, Ltd.
PO Box 764
Usa River,
Arusha
www.serengetipridesafaris.com
T. +255 (0) 785 353 534
E. info@SerengetiPrideSafaris.com

Kilimanjaro Mountain resort
Kyalla - Marangu West
PO Box 301,
Kilimanjaro National Park
www.kilimountresort.com

Rivertrees
near Usa-River village
Arusha
www.rivertrees.com

Arusha Coffee Lodge
Dodoma Road,
Arusha
www.elewanacollection.com
T. +255 (0) 272500630
E. info@elewana.com

Zanzibar

Zanzibar Tourist Information
www.zanzibar-island.com

Pure Zanzibar
www.purezanzibar.com
T. +44 (0) 1227 753180
E. info@purezanzibar.com

Saadani National Park
Tourist Information
Bagamoyo Tanzania
www.saadanipark.org
T. +255 (0)21 621276144

Silk Route Restaurant
Stone Town,
Zanzibar
Open daily 12.00–15.00 and
18.30–23.00
T. +255 (0) 78 687 9696

Mercury's
Stone Town
Zanzibar
T. +255 (0) 77 741 3081
Open daily 12.00–0.00

Tower Top
236 Hurumzi Hotel
Stone Town, Zanzibar
T. +255 (0)24 223 2784

Baraza
PO Box 2284,
Zanzibar
www.baraza-zanzibar.com
T. +255 (0) 774 440 330
E. info@baraza-zanzibar.com

Essque Zalu Zanzibar
PO Box 3151
Zanzibar
www.essquehotels.com
T. +255 (0) 778 683 960
E. sales@essquehotels.com

Serena Inn Stone Town
Stone Town, Zanzibar
www.serenahotels.com
T.+255 (0) 242233567
E. zanzibar@serena.co.tz

Pemba

Fundu Lagoon
T. +44 (0)870 2406008
(UK reservations)
www.fundulagoon.com
T. +255 (0) 7774 38 668
E. info@fundulagoon.com

Cotswold Outdoor
for all your outdoor clothing and equipment needs

TRAVEL
Gearing up for travel any time is easy with the full range of clothing, luggage and accessories available all year round.

OUTDOOR
All your outdoor needs are covered with waterproof jackets & trousers, fleeces & rucksacks.

FOOTWEAR
From sandals to mountain boots there are dozens of options in footwear and we also offer a free expert boot fitting service.

ACTIVE
Lightweight performance gear to offer you maximum comfort in high-energy activities and warmth when needed.

CLIMBING
Bouldering or climbing, beginner or expert. Our massive range will appeal to everyone.

CASUAL
A range of casual clothing for getting comfy after a strenuous day or just for everyday wear.

CAMPING
Sleeping bags, tents and camping accessories that will have you sleeping under the stars in comfort on family trips and expeditions alike.

**From Aberdeen to Truro,
Ipswich to Carmarthen we're never far away**

60+ stores nationwide | 0844 557 7755 | cotswoldoutdoor.con

Snapshot of where to go and when...

February Half Term

February half terms falls in mid-February and is generally 1 week.

- **Nature + Wildlife** – safari of a lifetime, see the migration in the Serengeti National Park
- **Adventure** – Learning to ski in style in Valais and stay in a Swiss lodge
- **Reflect + Re-new** – Chill out and dine at the desert resort in Ras al-Khaimah

Easter Holidays

The Easter holidays separating the spring term and the summer term, are generally 2 weeks.

- **Education + Hands on** – Camping, looking after lambs and learning about wildlife in Northern Ireland
- **History + Culture** – enjoy a short city break in Dublin
- **Food + Discovery** – Head to the North Male Atoll, Maldives for a week of sun, sand and snorkelling

May Half Term

May half term falls in late May or early June and is generally 1 week.

- **Food + Discovery** – explore the marvellous Lycian coastline on a Turkish Gullet
- **Action + Adventure** – learn to surf and explore the coastline of Ireland
- **History + Culture** – spend a week exploring the sights of Malta

Summer Holidays

The British summer holidays which begin in late July, usually consisting of 6 weeks mark the end and beginning of the UK school year.

- **Reflect + Re-new** – pack your beach bag, bucket and spade and head to the Island of Gozo
- **Action + Adventure** – trek Machu Picchu and marvel at the impressive Inca ruins
- **Education + Hands on** – explore the mystic Zanzibar, stay in a beach hut and learn to scuba dive

October Half Term

October half term falls in late October and is generally 1 week.

- **History + Culture** - explore the secrets of Istanbul's famous souks and museums
- **Action + Adventure** – tackle Africa's largest peak 'Kilimanjaro', a 7 day hike to the summit
- **Food + Discovery** – check-in to a top hotel in Abu Dhabi, and take a glimpse into the emirates past

Christmas Holidays

The Christmas holidays separating the autumn term and spring term are generally 2 weeks.

- **Adventure + Adventure** – drive across the desert in a jeep and seek some heat in Dubai
- **History + Culture** – visit the Christmas markets and sights in Zurich
- **Education + Hands on** – swim, snorkel and learn about Maldivian culture in South Male Atoll, Maldives

If you are looking for more inspiration, then visit us
www.luxurybackpackers.com

Acknowledgements

Adventure Index

We would like to sincerely thank the following people and organisations for their help in producing this book.

Stephanie Meadows, Kerry Dennison, Pauline Dennison, Chris Capstick, Rebecca Pride (The Adventure Company), Orient Express, Dee Gallagher (Spice PR), The Ice House, Tourism Ireland, Ursula Von Platen (Kempinski), One&Only Resorts, Waldorf Astoria Beach House Maldives, Feather Down Farm Days, Clark V Kays, Christine Rodgers (National Trust), Charlotte Tidball (Virgin Limited Edition), Vanessa Flack (Dolder Grand), GrifCo, PRCO, Catherine O'Dolan (Junior Magazine), Small Luxury Hotels, Relais & Châteaux, NCT, Sarah Gordon (Travel Mail), Justine Roberts Mumsnet, Cara Sayer (Snoozeshade), Rachel Jones (Totseat), Cotswold Outdoor, Susan Lord (Green People), Fourbgb, Catherine Fairweather (Harpers Bazaar), ADTA, Results PR, Harvey Nichols, Kristina Roe (Responsible Travel), Joanna Marsh (Turkey Tourism UK), Visit Maldives, Switzerland Tourism, Anna Catchpole (Virgin Atlantic), Hill and Dean PR, Beth Cooper PR

ISBN 978-0-9557397-5-0
Published by Luxury Backpackers Ltd 2011 in the UK

© 2011 Luxury Backpackers Ltd

Luxury Backpackers Ltd Reg. No. 5661479
Address for Luxury Backpackers can be found on
www.luxurybackpackers.com

Luxury Backpackers, Adventures in Style and the
Luxury Backpackers Logo are trademarks of Luxury
Backpackers Ltd and are registered in the UK Patent
& Trademark Office. Luxury Backpackers Ltd makes
every effort to ensure that all our books and company
stationery are made from 100% recycled paper sources
from post-consumer waste.

Printed in the UK

Designer: Stephanie Meadows